Keto Diet Air Fryer Cookbook

Fried Food is No Longer a Problem. Little Oil, you Lose Weight and a Lot of Health!

Jhonson J. Willett

© Copyright 2018 by Jhonson J. Willett

All rights reserved.

The following eBook is reproduced below with the goal of providing information that is as accurate and as reliable as possible. Regardless, purchasing this eBook can be seen as consent to the fact that both the publisher and the author of this book are in no way experts on the topics discussed within, and that any recommendations or suggestions made herein are for entertainment purposes only. Professionals should be consulted as needed before undertaking any of the action endorsed herein.

This declaration is deemed fair and valid by both the American Bar Association and the Committee of Publishers Association and is legally binding throughout the United States.

Furthermore, the transmission, duplication, or reproduction of any of the following work, including precise information, will be considered an illegal act, irrespective of whether it is done electronically or in print. The legality extends to creating a secondary or tertiary copy of the work or a recorded copy and is only allowed with the express written consent of the Publisher. All additional rights are reserved.

The information in the following pages is broadly considered to be a truthful and accurate account of facts, and as such any inattention, use, or misuse of the information in question by the reader will render any resulting actions solely under their purview. There are no scenarios in which the publisher or the original author of this work can be in any fashion deemed liable for any hardship or damages that may befall them after undertaking information described herein.

Additionally, the information found on the following pages is intended for informational purposes only and should thus be considered universal. As befitting its nature, the information presented is without assurance regarding its continued validity or interim quality. Trademarks that mentioned are done without written consent and can in no way be considered an endorsement from the trademark holder.

Table of Contents

Introduction 9
Chapter 1: What is the Keto Diet? 11
    The Right Keto Plan 11
    How the Keto Plan Works 12
    The Process 12
    Steps to Achieve Ketosis 13
        Step 1: Lower Your Carb Consumption 13
        Step 2: Increase the Healthy Fat Intake to Your Diet Plan 13
        Step 3: Incorporate Coconut Oil Into Your Keto Diet Plan 14
        Step 4: Maintain Protein Intake 14
        Step 5: Test the Ketone Levels & Adjust the Diet Plan 15
    Tips to Transition Into the Ketogenic Diet 16
    How Long Before Ketosis 17
    How to Know When You are in Ketosis 17
        Ketosis and Your Sleep Patterns 17
        Bad Breath Happens 18
        Lowered Appetite 18
        Pungent Urine Smells 19
        Thirst is Increased 19
        Digestive Issues 19
        Other Possible Side Effects 20
Chapter 2: Benefits of the Ketogenic Diet 21
Chapter 3: Keto Diet Food List & Foods to Avoid 24
    Protein Products 24

Dairy Products 24
Vegetables 25
Healthy Fats 26
Pantry Items 26
Foods to Limit 26

Chapter 4: What is an Air Fryer? 29
Tips for the Air Fryer 29
Proof you Should own an Air Fryer 30

Chapter 5: Temperatures & Cooking Times 32
Category 1: Vegetables 32
Category 2: Chicken: Various Cuts: 33
Category 3: Lamb & Pork 34
Category 4: Fish & Seafood 34
Category 5: Beef Choices 35
Category 6: Frozen Foods 35

Chapter 6: How to Lose Weight 36
Cortisol Levels—Exercise & the Keto Diet 36
Exercise to Meet Success 36

Chapter 7: Breakfast Choices 38
Air Bread & Egg Butter 38
Egg Butter 39
Avocado Egg Boats 40
Avocado Muffins 41
Bacon & Cheese Muffins 42
Bacon & Hot Dog Omelet 44
Chicken Hash 45

Chicken Strips 46

Delicious Eggs, Ham, & Spinach 47

Egg Cups With Bacon 48

Egg Pizza 50

Eggs in a Zucchini Nest 51

Ham Hash 52

Herbed Eggs 53

Mushroom, Onion, & Cheese Frittata 54

Poached Eggs 55

Sausage & Turkey Patties 56

Scrambled Pancake Hash 57

Spinach Frittata 58

Tofu Egg Muffins 59

Western Omelet 60

Avocado Fries 62

Avocado Bacon Fries 63

Baby Corn 64

Baked Tomatoes With Feta & Pesto 65

Carrots, Zucchini, & Yellow Squash 66

Cheesy Asparagus 67

Chili Cumin Squash 68

Crispy Black-Eyed Peas 69

Crispy & Spicy Cauliflower 70

Curried Cauliflower Florets 71

Daikon Fries 72

Easy Tofu 73

Grilled Cheesy Corn 74

Lemony Green Beans 75

Onion Rings 76

Roasted Cauliflower With Raisins & Nuts 77

Tawa Vegetables 78

Zucchini Fries 79

Chapter 9: Appetizers 81

Bacon-Wrapped Chicken 81

Bacon-Wrapped Prawns 82

Charred Shishito Peppers 83

Cheese Balls 84

Herbal Chicken Wings 85

Hot Chicken Wings 86

Onion & Cheese Nuggets 88

Semolina Veggie Cutlets 89

Spring Rolls 90

Sweet & Sour Chicken Skewers 92

Zucchini Roll-Ups 93

Snacks 94

Onion Pakora 96

Pineapple Sticks With Yogurt Dip 97

Roasted Cashews 98

Spiced Nuts 99

Sweet Potato Chips 100

Burrito 101

Beef & Potato 102

Beef Roll-Ups 103

Beef Stew 104

Beef & Bacon Taco Rolls 105

Cheeseburger Patties 106

Chicken Curry 107

Corn Beef 108

Grilled Cheese 109

Herbed Shredded Beef 110

Mozzarella Turkey Rolls 111

Pita Bread Pizza 112

Roast Beef for Sandwiches 113

Salmon Croquettes 114

Stuffed Mushrooms 115

Chapter 11: Dinner Choices 117

Fish & SeafoodCoconut Shrimp 117

Chapter 12: Dessert Temptations 126

Blackberry Pie 126

Cheesecake 128

Chocolate Chip Cookies 129

Green Avocado Pudding 131

Sweet Bacon Cookies 132

Conclusion 133

Introduction

I am so glad you took time out of your busy schedule to download a copy of the *Keto Diet Air Fryer Cookbook: Fried Food is No Longer a Problem. Little oil, you lose weight and a lot of health!* Thank you for doing so. The following chapters will discuss some of the many different ways you can stay in tune with your keto diet plan with the aid of your Air Fryer.

The keto diet plan goes by many different names such as the low-carb diet, keto diet, and the low-carbohydrate diet & high-fat (LCHF) diet plan. Your liver produces ketones that are used as energy to provide adequate levels of proteins similar to other low-carbohydrate diet techniques. The process known as ketosis is natural and happens every day—no matter the total of carbs consumed.

In 1924, Dr. Russell Wilder worked for the Mayo Clinic and became well-known when he formulated the keto plan that was used as part of an epilepsy therapy treatment plan at that time. He had a huge interest in the plan because he also suffered from epilepsy. The plan became known for its other effects that helped in weight loss and many other ailments.

The ketosis dieting technique was set aside in the 1940s because "improved" methods were discovered for the treatment of epilepsy. However, during that time—approximately 30% of the cases using the alternate plan had failed.

Hot air frying is a cooking method that allows grilling, frying, and roasting without the use of large amounts of oil. You enjoy that deep-fried taste and texture without the overuse of oil.

Several types are on the market dating back to the commercial basket hot air fryer invented in 1999, the paddle-type Actifry unit in 2006, and lastly—the domestic basket hot air fryer designed in 2010 with the improved Philips Air Fryer.

Just when you believed there was no alternative and fried foods were barred from your life forever, you can now enjoy your favorite fried foods as a part of your daily diet. You can experiment with more types of oil including grapeseed oil, walnut oil, and avocado oil. These are healthier oils that make the sky's the limit for tasty fried foods you can now enjoy with your new Air Fryer.

Low-fat air fryer cooking will provide you with foods prepared with the circulation of hot air. All of the excess fat can drip down into a tray below the cooking basket. The compact air fryer allows you to set the cooking temperature and timer. All you need to do is wait for the beep, and your food is ready for the table.

You won't need to a have a dirty workspace, since there is no huge mess to clean. Cooking food in the fryer is fast, safe, and healthy any time—day or night.

One Quick Note: You might need to use a sling when lowering a pan into the air fryer. Fold a section of aluminum foil into a strip into lengths long enough to fit under the pan and not be burned in the process. It should be cut in strips of 2 x 24 inches.

Let's begin!

Chapter 1: What is the Keto Diet?

The Right Keto Plan

- *Plan # 1*: You can choose from the standard ketogenic diet (SKD) that consists of high-fat, moderate protein and is extremely low in carbs. You will stay within the limits of 20 to 50 grams of net carbohydrates daily.

- *Plan # 2*: The cyclical ketogenic diet or CKD is created with 5-keto days trailed by two high-carb days. You would consume low carbs for a few days and then consume high carbs for 24 to 48 hours (450 to 600 grams daily). This is an excellent plan for athletes and bodybuilders.

- *Plan # 3*: The high-protein ketogenic diet is very similar to the standard keto plan; with one exception, it has more protein.

- *Plan # 4*: The targeted keto diet, which is also called TKD, will provide you with a plan to add carbs to your diet during the times when you're working out. The plan is modified from the SKD plan, but you may need an additional intake of carbs since you are "fast-digesting" carbohydrates prior to workout times (30-60 minutes). The plan is best for individuals who maintain a high-activity lifestyle such as athletes. You will need to maintain 25 to 50 grams or less of net carbs.

These are the basic plans to get you on the right path.

How the Keto Plan Works

The keto diet will limit the volume of carbs you consume. Much of your fuel for the day is derived from *fat* converted to *ketones*. When you have the protein, carbohydrates, and fat ratio monitored by the diet plan such as shown in this cookbook, you are well on the way to a successful diet strategy and achieving ketosis.

You will not be overeating with large portions of protein. You won't eliminate fat or carbs that make it a useful and safe diet plan for fat loss. If you take the approach of eating less, without considering your diet, you will be losing essential minerals and vitamins you need daily—which can result in muscle spasms, fatigue, insomnia, mental fogginess, hunger, headaches, irritability, and emotional depression. You can also lose valuable muscle mass, not just the pounds you intended to drop.

By using the lower carb keto plan, you can reduce your carbohydrates and calorie counts and nurture your body with the suitable amount of water, meat, eggs, fish, veggies, nuts, as well as high-quality oils that create fat loss minus the unpleasant side effects.

The Process

When the glycerol and fatty acid molecules are released, the ketogenesis process begins, and acetoacetate is produced. The Acetoacetate is converted to two types of ketone units:

- **Acetone:** This is mostly excreted as waste but can also be metabolized into glucose. This is the reason individuals on a ketogenic diet will experience a distinctive smelly breath.

- **Beta-hydroxybutyrate or BHB:** Your muscles will convert the acetoacetate into BHB that will fuel your brain after you have been on the keto diet for a short time.

Steps to Achieve Ketosis

Step 1: Lower Your Carb Consumption

The most important element in achieving ketosis is a very low-carbohydrate diet. Your cells normally use the sugar/glucose as the main fuel source, but most of your cells can also use other sources of fuel such as fatty acids as well as ketones.
When the carb intake is lowered, the levels of the insulin hormone decline that allows the fatty acids to be released from fat storage in your body.

Step 2: Increase the Healthy Fat Intake to Your Diet Plan

Forget the old sayings of it has too much fat. Consuming plenty of "healthy fats" can help boost your ketone levels. The lowered carbohydrate intake teams up with the high fats to produce ketosis. If you are using the ketogenic diet for weight loss, you can also achieve 60 to 80% of your calories from fat. *Note:* The classic diet plan for epilepsy is higher with 85 to 90% of the calories from fat.

It is important to use high-quality food sources since you are consuming such a large percentage of your diet from fat intake. Consider using these good fats for your cooking needs: butter, coconut oil, avocado oil, tallow, and lard. You will soon discover how many high-fat foods are low in carbs, but you still need to count them to prevent losing the ketosis state.

Step 3: Incorporate Coconut Oil Into Your Keto Diet Plan

The oil is also used as one of the best ways to improve ketone levels in people with nervous system disorders, such as those with Alzheimer's disease.

Medium-chain triglycerides (MCTs) are components of coconut oil and will speed up the ketosis process. Unlike many other fats, the MCTs are absorbed rapidly and are used for immediate energy—resulting in conversion to ketones. The oil contains four types of these fats, 50% of which comes from the lauric acid. Research has indicated the higher percentage may produce sustained ketosis levels because it is metabolized more gradual than other MCTs.

Add coconut oil slowly to your diet because it can cause some stomach cramping or diarrhea. You will need to adjust the amounts. Begin with one teaspoon daily and work it up to two to three tablespoons over the span of a week.

Step 4: Maintain Protein Intake

You must supply your liver with amino acids that can be used for making new glucose (gluconeogenesis). Your liver produces the glucose for the cells and organs in your body that cannot use ketones as fuel. This includes portions of the brain, kidneys, and red blood cells.

Protein also maintains muscle mass when the carb intake is lowered, especially during a weight loss program. Think of it in simple terms; excessive protein intake may suppress ketone production, whereas consuming too little can lead to muscle mass loss.

Step 5: Test the Ketone Levels & Adjust the Diet Plan

Maintaining ketosis is an individual process, and you need to be sure you are achieving your goals. The levels of acetone, acetoacetate, and beta-hydroxybutyrate can be measured in your breath, urine, and blood.

You can use a Ketonix meter to measure your breath. You breathe into the meter, and a coded color will flash to show your levels of ketosis.

You can also measure the ketones with a blood ketone meter that works similar to a glucose meter. Add a small drop of blood on a testing strip and insert the tab into the meter. It will indicate the amount of beta-hydroxybutyrate in your bloodstream. This process has been researched as a valid indicator of the current ketosis levels. Unfortunately, the strips are expensive.

Test your urine for acetoacetates. The strip is dipped into the urine that will change the color of the strip. The various shades of purple and pink indicate the levels of the ketones. The darker the color on the testing strip, the higher the level of ketones. The major benefit is that they are inexpensive. The most effective time to test is early in the morning after a ketogenic diet dinner the previous evening. You should use one or more of these methods to indicate whether you need to adjust your intake of foods to remain in ketosis.

Two elements that occur when your body doesn't need the glucose:

- **The Stage of Lipogenesis:** If there is a sufficient supply of glycogen in your liver and muscles, any excess is converted to fat and stored.

- **The Stage of Glycogenesis:** The excess of glucose converts to glycogen and is stored in the muscles and liver. Research indicates that only about half of your energy used daily can be saved as glycogen.

Your body will have no more food (similar to when you are sleeping) making your body burn the fat to create ketones. Once the ketones break down the fats, which generate fatty acids, they will burn-off in the liver through beta-oxidation. Therefore, when you no longer have a supply of glycogen or glucose, ketosis begins and will use the consumed/stored fat as energy.

The Internet provides you with a keto calculator at "keto-calculator.ankerl.com." You can check your levels when you want to know what essentials your body needs during the course of your dieting plan or afterward. You will document your personal information such as height and weight. The calculator will provide you with the essential math.

Tips to Transition Into the Ketogenic Diet

It is a challenging process when you make a choice to change to a low-carb lifestyle. It takes a lot of willpower to refuse the sugary treats your family and friends can consume and not gain an ounce of body fat. However, you will be ahead of the game plan by using some of these suggestions. The keto plan works, and you can use it whether you are at home or on-the-go. These are the guidelines:

- **Count the Carbs:** In today's society, almost every consumable product purchased has the nutrient labeling on the package. Check them before you take them home. Take a bit of extra time when you plan a shopping adventure. It is essential to check the panels on every item to keep the ketosis in line. It might be a complicated process at first, but it is worth the effort.

- **Market Time:** When you go to the supermarket, take your new skills and a grocery list and search the labels.

- **Control the Kitchen:** One of the easiest ways to stay on your plan is to remove the temptations. Remove the candy, bread, pasta, rice, and sugary sodas you have supplied in your kitchen. If you live alone, this is an easy task. It is a bit more challenging if you have a family. The diet will also be useful for them if you plan your meals using some of the recipes included in this book.

- **Journalize:** Keep a journal/log of everything you eat. If you cheat, that has to count also. It will be a reminder of your indulgence, but it will help keep you in line. Others may believe you are obsessed with the plan, but it is your health and well-being that you are improving.

How Long Before Ketosis

When you fast, the hormones in your body will change. The keto plan is similar to this process. You could achieve ketosis in just a couple of days once you have used up all of your stored glycogen. It can take a month, a week, or just a few days. It all depends on which type of plan you choose (discussed earlier). Your protein and carbohydrate intake will determine the time. Exercise also plays a vital role.

How to Know When You are in Ketosis

Whether you have taken any tests to discover your ketosis status, your body will exhibit physical signs to prompt you. You may have a loss of appetite, increased thirst, have bad breath, or notice a stronger urine smell. These are all clues from your body.

Ketosis and Your Sleep Patterns

After you have a good night of sleep, your body is in ketosis since you have fasted for over 8 hours, you are on the way to burning ketones. If you are new to the high-fat and low-carb dieting, the optimal fat-burning state takes time. Your body has depended on bringing in carbs and glucose; it will not readily give up carbs and start to crave saturated fats.

The restless night is also a normal side effect. Vitamin supplements can sometimes remedy the problem that can be caused by a lowered insulin and serotonin level. For a quick fix; try one-half of a tablespoon of fruit spread and a square of chocolate.

Bad Breath Happens

You may notice a metallic or fruity taste with an odor similar to nail polish remover. This is the by-product of acetoacetic acid (acetone) that is an obvious indication. You may also experience a drier mouth. These changes are normal as a side effect as your body processes these high-fat foods.

Once you are accustomed to the ketogenic dieting techniques, the bad breath symptoms will pass. If you are socializing, try a diet soda or a no-sugar drink. Sugar-free gum is also a quick fix. Always check the nutrition labels for carbohydrate facts; you may be surprised. These are not allowed on the keto diet because they reduce ketones. Therefore, only use it temporarily. If you are at home, just grab the toothbrush.

Lowered Appetite

When you reduce your carbs and proteins, you will be increasing your fat intake. The reduced appetite comes from the multitude of fibrous veggies, fats, and satiating nutrients provided in the new diet.

The "full" factor is a huge benefit to the ketogenic plan. It will give you one less thing to worry about—being hungry.

Pungent Urine Smells

With the high acetone levels, your urine is also a strong clue to ketosis. There is no reason for concern; it's just your body adjusting to the new status.

Thirst is Increased

Fluid retention is increased when you are consuming carbohydrates. Once the carbs are flushed away, water weight is lost. You counterbalance by increasing the water intake since you are probably dehydrated.

The keto diet requires you to drink more water because you are storing carbs. If you are dehydrated, your body can use the stored carbs to restore hydration. When you're in ketosis, the carbs are removed, and your body doesn't have the water reserves. If you have tried other diets, you might have been dehydrated, but the higher carbohydrate counts stopped you from being thirsty.

Thus, the keto state is a diuretic state, so drink plenty of water daily.

Digestive Issues

You have made a huge change in your diet overnight; it's expected you may have problems including constipation or diarrhea when you first start the keto diet. Each person is different, and it will depend on what foods you have chosen to eat to increase your fiber intake using various vegetables.

You may experience issues because your fiber intake may be too high in comparison to your previous diet. Try reducing certain "new" foods until the transitional phase of keto is concluded. It should clear up with time.

You may be lacking beneficial bacteria. Try consuming fermented foods to increase your probiotics and aid digestion. You can benefit from B vitamins, omega-3 fatty acids, and beneficial enzymes as well.

Other Possible Side Effects

Induction Flu: The diet can make you irritable, nauseous, a bit confused, lethargic, and possibly suffer from a headache. Several days into the plan should remedy these effects. If not, add one-half of a teaspoon of salt to a glass of water and drink it to help with the side effects. You may need to do this once a day for about the first week, and it could take about 15 to 20 minutes before it helps. It will go away!

Constipation: During the ketogenic plan you must drink plenty of water or you could easily become constipated because of dehydration. The low carbs contribute to the issue. Eat the right veggies and add a small amount of salt to your food to help with the movements. If all else fails, try some *Milk of Magnesia*.

Leg Cramps: The loss of magnesium (a mineral) can be a demon and create a bit of pain with the onset of the keto diet plan changes. With the loss of the minerals during urination, you could experience bouts of cramps in your legs.

Heart Palpitations: You may begin to feel "fluttery" as a result of dehydration or because of an insufficient intake of salt. Try to make adjustments, but if you don't feel better quickly, you should seek emergency care.

Chapter 2: Benefits of the Ketogenic Diet

The ketogenic diet is an excellent plan and aids in some of the following illnesses:

- **Improved Thinking Skills:** Your brain is approximately 60% fat by weight. Therefore, you might become confused as you consume high-fat foods. By increasing your fatty foods intake, you will have better chances to better your mind. It can maintain itself and work at full capacity.

- **Obesity and Overweight People**: Many individuals exceed what is considered healthy figures when it comes to weight. It is imperative to use the keto diet plan to get started on the right path for weight loss.

- **Acne:** By eating fewer processed foods and less sugar, your insulin levels will be lowered, and the acne should improve.

- **Alzheimer's Disease:** The disease's progression can be slowed and the symptoms reduced with the keto plan.

- **Cancer:** Several types of cancer and slow tumor growths are being treated using the keto diet.

- **Prediabetes and Diabetes:** Excess fat is removed with the keto plan, which is what is linked to prediabetes, type-2 diabetes, and metabolic syndrome. In one study, insulin sensitivity was improved by 75%. Similar results with type-

2 diabetes patients indicated that out of 21 participants, seven were successful in eliminating all of the medications related to diabetes.

In another one-week study, individuals who were overweight with type-2 diabetes who limited their intake to 21 or fewer grams daily experienced urinary ketone excretion levels that were 27 times higher than their baseline levels.

- **Epilepsy:** Reductions from seizures have occurred in children who use the ketogenic diet. The therapeutic keto diet used for epilepsy often restricts the carbs to fewer than 15 grams of carbs daily to further drive up the ketone levels. Don't try this unless you have the supervision of a medical professional.

- **Gum Disease and Tooth Decay:** The pH balance in your mouth is influenced by sugar intake. Your gum issues could subside after about three months on a keto diet plan. You will be consuming healthier foods.

- **Lower Blood Pressure:** A low-carbohydrate diet is an excellent way to lower blood pressure scores. It is also advisable to speak with your physician about lowering your meds while on the plan. If you begin to feel dizzy, that is one of the first signs the lack of carbs is working. You are headed in the right direction.

- **Improvement of Your Cholesterol Profile:** An arterial buildup is generally associated with the triglyceride and cholesterol levels, which have been proven to improve with the keto diet plan.

- **Joint Pain and Stiffness:** Grain-based foods are eliminated from your diet on the keto plan. It is believed the grains can be one of the biggest causes of pain or chronic illness. After all, it has been said before, "no pain, no grain."

- **Lack of Hunger:** The enormous benefit occurs because fat is naturally more satisfying than just carbs. You just need to wait a little longer to become satiated after a meal. The high carbs will cause the full state to last longer.

Ketosis is used to help you drop extra pounds and burn body fat using healthy eating practices. Proteins will fuel your body to burn the fat, which in turn, ketosis will maintain your muscles and make you less hungry.

Your body will remain healthy and work as it should. If you don't consume enough carbs from your food, your cells will begin to burn fat for the necessary energy instead. Your body will switch over to ketosis for its energy source as you cut back on your calories and carbs.

Chapter 3: Keto Diet Food List & Foods to Avoid

You can prepare almost any meal if you have the right items in the pantry. By having the ingredients in the refrigerator, freezer, or cabinets, you can always stay on track. Begin with these items:

Protein Products

The keto plan focuses on quality proteins, not carbohydrates. You will see many items listed as a starting point.

- Tuna: Fresh & canned
- Salmon: Fresh wild caught salmon—portioned in bags to freeze
- Eggs
- Shrimp
- Fresh nuts: Macadamia, sesame seeds, flax seeds, chia seeds, etc.
- Turkey: Breasts & ground turkey
- Pork Chops
- Chicken: Thighs, breasts, drumsticks, & ground chicken
- Beef: Flank steak, chuck roast, sirloin, and lean ground beef
- Venison: This is a good choice since it is lean and vegetarian-raised meat.

Dairy Products

It is important to maintain your health using dairy products. It is best to choose fresh/raw or organic milk products. You can also add additional protein and calcium using nondairy products such as cashew or almond milk. Keep these in the fridge:

- Heavy cream
- Butter
- Cream cheese
- Sour cream
- Ghee
- Parmesan cheese
- Sharp cheddar cheese

Vegetables

Many of the vegetables have a lot of carbohydrates. You will want to consider these:

- Asparagus
- Broccoli
- Cauliflower
- Onions
- Bell pepper
- Cabbage
- Lettuce
- Tomatoes—limited
- Parsnips
- Radishes
- Bell Peppers
- Squash
- Peas
- Spinach
- Squash
- Turnip
- Zucchini

Healthy Fats

To achieve success on the ketogenic diet, you need fats. These are some of those:

- Avocado
- Extra-virgin olive oil (EVOO)
- Sesame, avocado, and coconut oil
- Flaxseed oil
- Coconut flakes
- Olives

Pantry Items

These are some of the favorites to use while on the ketogenic diet:

- Coconut flour
- Quinoa
- Splenda & Stevia
- Sugar-free ketchup
- Sugar-free gelatin
- Unsweetened cocoa powder
- Yellow mustard
- Pickles (limit sweet or bread & butter)
- Natural nut butter—no sugar

Foods to Limit

You may use these sometimes but try to limit the amounts used. Always count for the extra carbs in your recipes. These are a few of the ones to use occasionally—if you have a craving:

- Agave Nectar: One teaspoon has 5 grams of carbs versus 4 grams of table sugar.

- Beans and Legumes: This group to avoid includes peas, lentils, kidney beans, and chickpeas. If you use them, be sure to count the carbs, protein, and fat content.

- Cashews and Pistachios: The high-carb content should be monitored for these yummy nuts.

- Fruits: Raspberries, blueberries, and cranberries contain a high-sugar content. In small portions, you can enjoy some strawberries, apples, or pears.

- Grains and Starches: Avoid all grain products including wheat-based items such as cereal, rice, or pasta.

- Hydrogenated Fats: Cold-pressed items should be avoided when using vegetable oils such as safflower, olive, soybean, or flax. Coronary heart disease has been linked to these fats that also include margarine.

- Sweet potatoes

- Potatoes and potato products

- Corn and corn products

- Alcohol Products: You need to limit the intake of your alcoholic drinks which will include the following:
    1. Beer
    2. Flavored liquor
    3. Cocktails
    4. Dry Wine
    5. Mixers: Soda, Juice, or Syrup

However, some of the professionals have discovered these might be acceptable:

- Rum: Choose the ones with zero carbs or sugar.
- Tequila: The agave plant is the source of tequila.
- Vodka: Check the carb content since it is usually produced (grain-based) from rye, potatoes, and wheat.
- Whiskey, Barley, corn, rye, and wheat are the grains used that have zero carbs or sugar.

Note: This doesn't promote you drinking alcohol, but it does produce ketones in the liver. Remember, it still needs to be consumed in small amounts to prevent any health issues.

You should also avoid sugar including these:

- Dextrose
- Corn syrup
- Fructose
- Honey Maltose
- Maple syrup

Chapter 4: What is an Air Fryer?

Tips for the Air Fryer

Tip #1 **Using**: Many premade packaged food items can be cooked using the Air Fryer. Each food may vary with its cooking time. As a guideline, reduce the cooking times by about 70% compared to times in a conventional oven.

Tip #2: While cooking smaller items such as fries or wings, you can make sure they are cooking evenly by shaking the basket several times during the cooking process.

Tip #3: It is important to pat food items dry if you have marinated or soaked them in to help eliminate splattering or excessive smoke.

Tip #4: It is tempting when you are in a rush to attempt to overload the Air Fryer. Don't put too much in the cooking basket at one time. You won't receive the best results if the air cannot make the 360° turns that make the cooker so unique.

Tip #5: Allow at least 3 minutes warm-up time each time you use the fryer so that it can reach its correct starting temperature.

Tip #6: When it comes to the time to clean the cooking basket, loosen any food particles remaining attached to the basket. Soak each of the attachments in a soapy water solution before scrubbing or placing it in the dishwasher.

Tip #7: If you use aluminum foil or parchment paper, leave a one-half-inch space around the bottom edge of the basket.

Tip #8: Cooking sprays are an excellent choice to spray on your food before cooking. You can also spray the mesh of the cooking basket to keep anything from sticking to its surface.

Proof you Should own an Air Fryer

Benefit #1: It is a beginner's treat. You can locate your favorite recipes and whip up a remarkable meal at home in half of the time. The machine does the hard work for you. All you need to do is "punch in" the temperature and time.

Benefit #2: The Fryer Needs Less Oil: It won't be necessary to add oil to the cooker if you have frozen products that are meant for baking. You only need to adjust the timer and cook. All of the excess fat will drip away into a tray beneath the basket.
You can cook whatever meats you enjoy and receive delicious and healthy results. You will understand this once you begin trying out some of these new recipes.

For example, you can cook French fries with a tablespoon of oil versus a vat of oil.

Benefit #3: No Oily Clean Up: You only need to remove the cooking bowl, drip pan, or the cooking basket. It is inside a cover that means you won't have oil vapor deposits on the walls, floors, or countertops.
You can use the dishwasher to clean the movable parts. You can also use a sponge to clean the bits of food that might be stuck to the AF surfaces.

Benefit #4: Purchase Less Oil: It is possible to splurge on the more expensive oils since you only use such a minimal amount.

Benefit #5: Multitasking Features: The Air Fryer is capable of functioning as so many products, whether you need an oven, a hot grill, a toaster, a skillet, or a deep fryer—it is your answer! It can be used for breakfast, lunch, dinner, desserts, and even snacks.

Benefit #6: Safety Functions: The machine will automatically shut down when the cooking time is completed. You will have less burned or overheated food items. The fryer will not slip because of the nonslip feet that help eliminate the risk of the machine from falling off of the countertop. The closed cooking system helps prevent burns from hot oil or other foods.

Now that you know how to avoid some of the pitfalls you may have with your new Air Fryer unit, you can begin planning which delicious treat you want to test first!

Chapter 5: Temperatures & Cooking Times

The times and temperatures mentioned in this segment are considered food that is flipped when the food is at its halfway point of the cooking time or if the basket is shaken to shuffle the ingredients a time or two.

Category 1: Vegetables

The following vegetables are prepared at 400°F:

- Asparagus—1-inch slices—5 min.
- Beets—whole—40 min.
- Broccoli—florets—6 min.
- Cauliflower—florets—12 min.
- Eggplant—1 ½-inch cubes—15 min.
- Green Beans—5 min.
- Mushrooms—sliced ¼-inch thick—5 min.
- Pearl Onions—10 min.
- Peppers—1-inch chunks—15 min.
- Small Baby Potatoes—1 ½ lb.—15 min.
- Potatoes—1-inch chunks—12 min.
- Whole Baked Potatoes—40 min.
- Squash—½ inch chunks—12 min.
- Cherry Tomatoes—4 min.
- Zucchini—½ inch sticks—12 min.

These veggies are best prepared at 380°F:

- Brussels Sprouts in halves—15 min.
- Carrots—½-inch slices—15 min.
- Parsnips—½-inch chunks—15 min.
- Baked Sweet Potato—30-35 min.

Other veggies:

- Corn on the Cob—390°F—6 min.
- Tomatoes—halved—350°F—10 min.

Category 2: Chicken: Various Cuts:

Prepared at 360°F:

- Tenders—8-10 min.
- Whole Chicken—6.5 lb.—1 ¼ hr.

Prepared at 370°F:

- Bone-In Breasts—1 ¼ lb.—25 min.
- Drumsticks—2 ½ lb.—20 min.

Prepared at 380°F:

- Boneless Breasts—4 oz.—12 min.
- Bone-In Thighs—2 lb.—22 min.
- Boneless Thighs—1 ½ lb.—18-20 min.
- Bone-In Legs—1 ¾ lb.—30 min.

Category 3: Lamb & Pork

Prepared at 360°F:

- Loin—2 lb. 55 min.

Prepared at 370°F:

- Tenderloin—1 lb.

Prepared at 380°F:

- Sausages—15 min.
- Rack of Lamb—1 ½ to 2 lb.—22 min.

Prepared at 400°F:

- Bone-In Pork Chops—1 inch/6.5 oz.—12 min.
- Regular Bacon—5-7 min.
- Bacon—Thick-Cut—6-10 min.
- Lamb Loin Chops—1-inch thick—8-12 min.

Category 4: Fish & Seafood

Prepared at 380°F:

- Salmon fillet—6 oz.—12 min.

Prepared at 400°F:

- Calamari—8 oz.—4 min.
- Fish Fillet—8 oz./1 inch—10 min.
- Swordfish Steak—10 min.
- Tuna Steak—7-10 min.
- Scallops—5-7 min.
- Shrimp—5 min.

Category 5: Beef Choices

Prepared at 370°F:

- Burger—4 oz.—16-20 min

Prepared at 380°F:

- Meatballs—1 inch—7 min.
- Meatballs—3 inches—10 min.

Prepared at 390°F.

- Beef—Eye-Round Roast—4 lb.—45-55 min.

Prepared at 400°F:

- Fillet Mignon—8 oz.—18 min.
- Flank Steak—1 ½ lb.—12 min.
- London Broil—2 lb.—20-28 min.
- Bone-In Rib Eye—1 inch—8 oz.—10-15 min.
- Sirloin Steaks—1 inch—12 oz.—9-14 min.

Category 6: Frozen Foods

The following food items are prepared at 400°F:

- Thin French Fries—2 oz.—14 min.
- Thick French Fries—17 oz.—18 min.
- Onion Rings—12 oz.—8 min.
- Mozzarella Sticks—11 oz.—8 min.
- Pot Stickers—10 oz.—8 min.
- Chicken Nuggets—12 oz.—10 min.
- Fish Fillets—½ inch—10 oz.—14 min.
- Fish Sticks—10 oz.—10 min.
- Breaded Shrimp—9 min.

Note: Remember, these are estimated times. Each Air Fryer may vary depending on the variations of a particular recipe.

Chapter 6: How to Lose Weight

The Air Fryer provides you with healthier food preparation options. The keto plan offers you the tools to achieve that by using the high-fat and low-carbohydrate diet plan as described. The elements discussed in this segment show how exercise also plays a major role in weight loss.

Cortisol Levels—Exercise & the Keto Diet

Firstly, you need to understand that cortisol is a hormone that is released from your adrenal gland in response to chemical signs or other stress signals. The release of cortisol in long workouts, such as jogging, and the adverse effects of the release of high doses of cortisol for weight loss are essential elements in your successful program. The hormone creates the fight-or-flight reaction as a result of the additional activity/stress during your workout.

Exercise to Meet Success

Short exercises of approximately 21 minutes daily have been scientifically proven to be more beneficial than longer workouts. For many years, trainers believed in sit-ups and push-ups with endless repetitions, but not today!

When you're working out on a treadmill or stationary bike, you're building up the cortisol in your body that is a stress hormone that helps burn fat. However, if you have a lot of exercises planned, your body will move into a protection mode. This mode will cause storage of fat around your midsection that can put you at risk for diabetes, heart disease, or possibly cancer.

The type of plan that will work for you is a high-intensity interval training (HIIT) technique. Workout in short intervals any time of the day you feel the need to get moving. You just need fast feet and high knee lifts to perform your exercises. After all, you are trying to push your heart to its maximum, not your biceps.

Chapter 7: Breakfast Choices

Air Bread & Egg Butter

Yields: 19 Servings
Total Time: 25 min.
Nutrition Facts: Cal.: 40 | Fat: 3.9 g | Prot.: 1.2 g | Net Carbs: 0.5 g

Ingredients for the Air Bread:

- 3 eggs
- 1 t. baking powder
- ¼ t. sea salt
- 1 c. almond flour
- ¼ c. butter

How to Prepare the Bread:

1. Soften the butter to room temperature. Whisk the eggs with a hand mixer. Combine the two and add the rest of the fixings to make a dough.
2. Knead the dough and cover with a tea towel for about 10 minutes.
3. Set the Air Fryer at 350°F.
4. Air fry the bread for 15 minutes. Check the center with a toothpick for doneness.
5. Remove the bread and let it cool down on a wooden board.
6. Slice and serve with your favorite meal or as it is.

Egg Butter

Yields: 4 Servings
Total Time: 17 min.
Nutrition Facts: Cal.: 164 | Fat: 8.5 g | Prot.: 3 g | Net Carbs: 2.67 g

Ingredients for the Egg Butter:

- 4 eggs
- 1 t. salt
- 4 tbsp. butter

How to Prepare:

1. Add a layer of foil to the Air Fryer basket and add the eggs. Cook at 320°F for 17 minutes. Transfer to an ice-cold water bath to chill.
2. Peel and chop the eggs and combine with the rest of the fixings. Mix well until it reaches a creamy texture.
3. Enjoy with your Air Fried Bread. Doesn't that sound heavenly?

Avocado Egg Boats

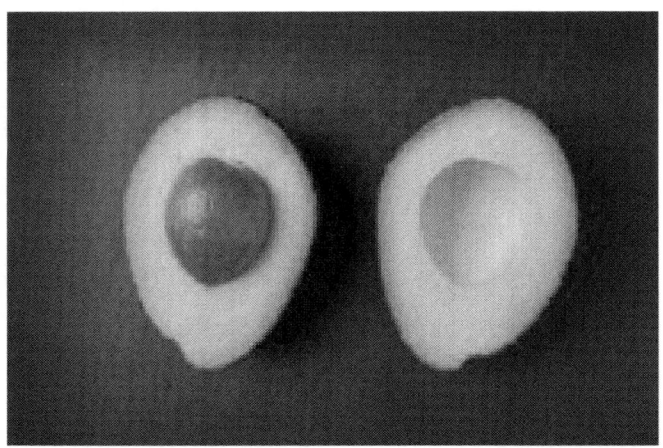

Yields: 2 Servings
Total Time: 16 min.
Nutrition Facts: Cal.: 288 | Fat: 26 g | Prot.: 7.6 g | Net Carbs: 9.4 g

Ingredients:

- 1 avocado—no pit
- 2 large eggs
- Freshly chopped chives and parsley—to your liking
- Pepper & Salt—to taste

How to Prepare:

1. Warm up the fryer to 350°F.
2. Remove the pit from the avocado. Slice and scoop out part of the flesh. Shake with the seasonings.
3. Add an egg to each half and place in the preheated Air Fryer for 6 minutes.
4. Remove and serve with some additional parsley and chives if desired.

Avocado Muffins

Yields: 7 Servings
Total Time: 30 min.
Nutrition Facts: Cal.: 133 | Fat: 12.4 g | Prot.: 2.2 g | Net Carbs: 2.9 g

Ingredients:

- 1 c. almond flour
- ½ t. baking soda
- 1 t. apple cider vinegar
- 1 egg
- 4 tbsp. butter
- 3 scoops stevia powder
- ½ c. pitted avocado
- 1 oz. melted dark chocolate

How to Prepare:

1. Preheat the Air Fryer to 355°F.
2. Whisk the almond flour, baking soda, and vinegar. Add the stevia powder and melted chocolate.
3. Whisk the egg in another container and add to the mixture along with the butter.
4. Peel, cube, and mash the avocado and add. Blend with a hand mixer to make the flour mixture smooth. Pour into the muffin forms (½ full). Cook for 9 minutes.
5. Lower the heat (340°F) and cook for 3 more minutes.
6. Chill before serving for the best results.

Bacon & Cheese Muffins

Yields: 6 Servings
Total Time: 45 min.
Nutrition Facts: Cal.: 251 | Fat: 20 g | Prot.: 12 g | Net Carbs: 6 g

Ingredients:

- 1 large egg
- 4 large slices of bacon
- 1 med. diced onion
- 2 tbsp. olive oil
- 2 t. baking powder
- 1 c. of each:
    - Milk
    - Shredded cheddar cheese
- 1 ½ c. almond flour
- 1 t. parsley
- Pepper and salt to taste
- Also Needed: 6 muffin tins to fit in the basket

How to Prepare:

1. Set the temperature on the Air Fryer to 356°F.
2. Prepare the bacon slices with a small amount of oil. Add the onion when it's about ¾ ready. Sauté and set aside when translucent. Drain on towels.
3. Mix the rest of the fixings and stir well. Add the onions and bacon.
4. Stir well and add the batter into 6 muffin holders. Add to the fryer basket for 20 minutes. Lower the heat for 10 minutes (320°F).
5. Serve and enjoy right out of the fryer.

Bacon & Hot Dog Omelet

Yields: 4 Servings
Total Time: 20 min.
Nutrition Facts: Cal.: 215 | Fat: 12 g | Prot.: 11 g | Net Carbs: 12 g

Ingredients:

- 2 small sliced onions
- 4 eggs
- 2 sliced hot dogs
- 1 slice of bacon—in pieces
- To Taste: Salt and pepper

How to Prepare:

1. Warm up the fryer (320°F) and combine all the fixings.
2. Pour the mixture into the baking tray. Air fry for 10 minutes. Serve.

Chicken Hash

Yields: 3 Servings
Total Time: 14 min.
Nutrition Facts: Cal.: 261 | Fat: 16.8 g | Prot.: 21 g | Net Carbs: 7.1 g

Ingredients:

- 7 oz. chicken fillet
- 6 oz. chopped cauliflower
- ½ yellow diced onion
- 1 chopped green pepper
- 1 tbsp. of each:
    - Water
    - Cream
- 1 t. black pepper
- 3 tbsp. butter

How to Prepare:

1. Program the Air Fryer to 380°F. Chop the cauliflower and add to a blender to make rice. Chop the chicken into bite-sized pieces and sprinkle with salt and pepper.
2. Prepare the veggies and combine the fixings.
3. Add the fryer basket and cook until done (6-7 minutes). Watch closely to prevent scorching.
4. Serve and enjoy.

Chicken Strips

Yields: 4 Servings
Total Time: 12 min.
Nutrition Facts: Cal.: 245 | Fat: 11.5 g | Prot.: 33 g | Net Carbs: 0.6 g

Ingredients:

- 1 lb. chicken fillets
- 1 t. paprika
- 1 tbsp. cream
- ½ t. salt & pepper

How to Prepare:

1. Dice the fillets into strips. Season to your liking with the salt and pepper.
2. Set the Air Fryer at 365°F and add the butter to the basket.
3. Arrange the strips in the basket and air fry for 6 minutes.
4. Flip the strips and cook for another 5 minutes.
5. When done, sprinkle with the cream and paprika. Serve warm.

Delicious Eggs, Ham, & Spinach

Yields: 4 Servings
Total Time: 30 min.
Nutrition Facts: Cal.: 190 | Fat: 13 g | Prot.: 15 g | Net Carbs: 3 g

Ingredients:

- 7 oz. sliced ham
- 2 ¼ c. spinach
- 4 t. cream milk
- 1 tbsp. olive oil
- 4 large eggs
- To Taste: Salt and pepper
- Also Needed:
    - 4 ramekins
    - Cooking spray
    - 1 Skillet

How to Prepare:

1. Set the fryer temperature to 356ºF. Spray the ramekins.
2. Warm up the oil in a skillet (medium heat) and sauté the spinach until wilted. Drain.
3. Divide the spinach and rest of the fixings in each of the ramekins.
4. Sprinkle with the salt and pepper. Bake until set (20 minutes).
5. Serve when they are to your liking.

Egg Cups With Bacon

Yields: 4 Servings
Total Time: 25 min.
Nutrition Facts: Cal.: 319 | Fat: 25.1 g | Prot.: 21.4 g | Net Carbs: 1.1 g

Ingredients:

- 4 eggs
- ½ t. of each:
    - Dried dill
    - Paprika
- ¼ t. salt
- 6 oz. bacon
- 1 tbsp. butter
- Also Needed: 4 ramekinso

How to Prepare:

1. Preheat the Air Fryer to 360°F.
2. Whisk the eggs and add the salt, paprika, and dried dill (a hand mixer is faster).
3. Coat the ramekins with butter. Slice the bacon and add to the cups.
4. Pour the egg fixings into the centers and air fry for 15 minutes.
5. Gently remove the cups and serve to a hungry crowd! You know the aromas are in the air!

Egg Pizza

Yields: 1 Serving
Total Time: 8 min.
Nutrition Facts: Cal.: 285 | Fat: 18 g | Prot.: 22 g | Net Carbs: 8 g

Ingredients:

- 2 eggs
- ½ t. of each:
    - Dried oregano
    - Dried basil
- 2 tbsp. shredded mozzarella cheese
- 4 thin slices of pepperoni
- Also Needed: 1 ramekin

How to Prepare:

1. Whisk the eggs with the oregano and basil.
2. Pour into the ramekin and top off with the pepperoni and cheese.
3. Arrange the ramekin in the air fryer. Prepare for 3 minutes and serve.

Eggs in a Zucchini Nest

Yields: 4 Servings
Total Time: 7 min.
Nutrition Facts: Cal.: 221 | Fat: 17.7 g | Prot.: 13.4 g | Net Carbs: 2.9 g

Ingredients:

- 8 oz. grated zucchini
- 4 t. butter
- ¼ t. sea salt
- ½ t. of each:
    - Black pepper
    - Paprika
- 4 eggs
- 4 oz. shredded cheddar cheese
- Also Needed: 4 ramekins

How to Prepare:

1. Preheat the Air Fryer at 356°F.
2. Grate the zucchini. Add the butter to the ramekins and add the zucchini in a nest shape. Sprinkle with the paprika, salt, and pepper.
3. Whisk the eggs and add to the nest, topping it off with the cheese.
4. Air fry for 7 minutes. Chill for 3 minutes and serve in the ramekin.

Ham Hash

Yields: 3 Servings
Total Time: 20 min.
Nutrition Facts: Cal.: 372 | Fat: 23.7 g | Prot.: 33.2 g | Net Carbs: 5.9 g

Ingredients:

- 10 oz. ham
- 5 oz. parmesan
- ½ onion
- 1 tbsp. butter
- 1 egg.
- 1 t. of each:
    - Ground black pepper
    - Paprika
- Also Needed: 3 ramekins

How to Prepare:

1. Preheat the fryer to 350°F.
2. Slice the ham into small strips and shred the parmesan cheese.
3. Peel and dice the onion. Lastly, whisk the egg and add to the rest of the fixings.
4. Sprinkle with the paprika, salt, and pepper. Add to the ramekins and sprinkle with the parmesan. Arrange the ramekins in the Air Fryer for 10 minutes.
5. When ready, remove from the fryer and scramble. Totally enjoy!

Herbed Eggs

Yields: 2 Servings
Total Time: 17 min.
Nutrition Facts: Cal.: 136 | Fat: 9.3 g | Prot.: 11.4 g | Net Carbs: 2.1 g

Ingredients:

- 4 hard-boiled eggs
- ½ t. sea salt
- 1 t. of each:
    - Dried parsley
    - Oregano
    - Paprika
- 1 tbsp. of each:
    - Chopped chives
    - Cream

How to Prepare:

1. Warm up the fryer to 320°F.
2. Add the eggs to the Air Fryer basket to cook for 17 minutes. Take from the fryer and add to cold water. Peel and slice into halves. Remove the yolks.
3. Combine the rest of the fixings (with the egg yolks) using a fork.
4. Fill the egg white halves with the mixture.
5. Serve and enjoy for breakfast or maybe a picnic.

Mushroom, Onion, & Cheese Frittata

Yields: 2 Servings
Total Time: 25 min.
Nutrition Facts: Cal.: 284 | Fat: 22 g | Prot.: 17 g | Net Carbs: 6 g

Ingredients:

- 1 tbsp. olive oil
- 2 c. sliced mushrooms
- 1 small sliced onion
- 3 eggs
- ½ c. grated cheese (50 g)
- Pinch of salt
- Also Needed: 1 Skillet

How to Prepare:

1. Program the Air Fryer to 320°F.
2. Warm up a skillet (medium heat) and add the oil.
3. Toss in the mushrooms and onions and sauté for about 5 minutes. Add to the Air Fryer.
4. Whisk the eggs with the salt and dump on top of the fixings in the fryer.
5. Sprinkle with the cheese and air fry for 10 minutes.
6. Take right out of the basket and serve. Yummy!

Poached Eggs

Yields: 1 Serving
Total Time: 5 min.
Nutrition Facts: Cal.: 72 | Fat: 5 g | Prot.: 6.3 g | Net Carbs: 0.4 g

Ingredients:

- 3 c. boiling water
- 1 large egg

How to Prepare:

1. Break the egg into a dish.
2. Add the boiling water to the Air Fryer basket.
3. Dump the egg into the water and place the basket in the fryer.
4. Prepare for 3 minutes. Use a slotted spoon and transfer the poached egg to a serving dish.

Sausage & Turkey Patties

Yields: 6 Servings
Total Time: 10 min.
Nutrition Facts: Cal.: 302 | Fat: 12.2 g | Prot.: 16.3 g | Net Carbs: 10.2 g

Ingredients:

- 1 t. olive oil
- 1 large chopped garlic clove
- 1 small diced onion
- To Taste: Pepper & Salt
- 1 tbsp. of each:
    - Chopped chives
    - Vinegar
- ¾ t. paprika
- 1 pinch of nutmeg
- 1 t. fennel seeds
- 1 lb. lean ground turkey

How to Prepare:

1. Heat up the Air Fryer (375°F).
2. Pour in ½ of the oil with the garlic and onion in the Air Fryer. Prepare for 1 minute and add the seeds. Place on a plate.
3. Combine the turkey, paprika, onion, pepper, salt, chives, nutmeg, and vinegar. Mix well and shape into patties.
4. Pour in the rest of the oil and air fry for 3 minutes.
5. Serve on keto-friendly buns.

Scrambled Pancake Hash

Yields: 7 Servings
Total Time: 9 min.
Nutrition Facts: Cal.: 178 | Fat: 13.3 g | Prot.: 4.4 g | Net Carbs: 10.7 g

Ingredients:

- 1 c. coconut flour
- 1 t. of each:
    - Ground ginger
    - Salt
    - Baking soda
- 1 tbsp. apple cider vinegar
- ¼ c. heavy cream
- 1 egg
- 5 tbsp. butter

How to Prepare:

1. Warm up the fryer to 400°F.
2. Combine the baking soda, flour, ginger, and salt in a mixing container.
3. In another dish, add the egg, butter, and cream. Blend well using a hand mixer. Combine the fixings and stir until smooth.
4. Carefully pour the mixture into the fryer basket tray and cook for 4 minutes.
5. Remove and scramble the hash. Continue cooking for 5 additional minutes.
6. Transfer to a serving platter and have a great start to your day.

Spinach Frittata

Yields: 2 Servings
Total Time: 20 min.
Nutrition Facts: Cal.: 159 | Fat: 9 g | Prot.: 14 g | Net Carbs: 6 g

Ingredients:

- 1/3 pkg. spinach
- 3 eggs
- 1 small minced onion
- Pepper & Salt to taste
- Mozzarella cheese

How to Prepare:

1. Warm up the Air Fryer to 356°F.
2. Spray the baking tray and add the onion. Air fry for 2 minutes.
3. Toss in the spinach and continue cooking for 5 minutes.
4. Whisk the eggs and cheese with the pepper and salt.
5. Bake until done (8 minutes). Serve piping hot!

Tofu Egg Muffins

Yields: 4 Servings
Total Time: 25 min.
Nutrition Facts: Cal.: 97 | Fat: 5 g | Prot.: 9 g | Net Carbs: 1 g

Ingredients:

- 1 small tofu chunk—in cubes
- 3 large eggs
- ¼ t. of each:
    - Sesame oil
    - Ground cumin
    - Ground coriander
    - Black pepper
- ½ t. soy sauce substitute—for example, keto-friendly is liquid aminos.
- A handful of each freshly chopped:
    - Spring onion
    - Coriander
- Also Needed: 4 muffin molds

How to Prepare:

1. Preheat the Air Fryer to 392°F (5 minutes).
2. Combine all of the fixings (omit the tofu). Whisk well.
3. Break the tofu into equal portions in the mold. Pour the mixture over each one.
4. Place in the Air Fryer for 10 minutes. Enjoy!

Western Omelet

Yields: 4 Servings
Total Time: 10 min.
Nutrition Facts: Cal.: 204 | Fat: 14.9g | Prot.: 14.8 g | Net Carbs: 4.3 g

Ingredients:

- 5 eggs
- 1 green pepper
- 1 ½ yellow diced onion
- 3 oz. shredded Parmesan cheese
- 3 tbsp. cream cheese
- 1 t. of each:
    - Olive oil
    - Dried cilantro
    - Dried oregano
    - Butter

Also Needed: 1 skillet

How to Prepare:

1. Whisk the eggs and add the cilantro, cream cheese, and oregano. Whisk gently and add the parmesan.
2. Warm up the fryer to 360°F (for a minute or so).
3. Pour the eggs into the Air Fryer basket and cook for 10 minutes.
4. Chop the onions and pepper. Prepare the skillet with the oil (medium heat) and sauté them for about 8 minutes.
5. When the eggs are done, add them to a serving platter and garnish with the sautéed veggies.

Chapter 8: Side Dishes & Veggies

You will surely find some of these veggie dishes delicious as they are when prepared and served right out of the fryer.

Avocado Fries

Yields: 2 Servings
Total Time: 15 min.
Nutrition Facts: Cal.: 176 | Fat: 14 g | Prot.: 3 g | Net Carbs: 10 g

Ingredients:

- 1 large avocado
- ½ c. breadcrumbs
- 1 lightly beaten egg
- ½ t. salt

How to Prepare:

1. Set the Air Fryer to 390°F. Peel, remove the pit, and slice the avocado.
2. Prepare 2 shallow dishes, one with the breadcrumbs and salt and one with a beaten egg.
3. First, dip the avocado into the egg—then the breadcrumbs.
4. Add to the fryer for 10 minutes.
5. Serve anytime you want a delicious side dish or an appetizer.

Avocado Bacon Fries

Yields: 2 Servings
Total Time: 35 min.
Nutrition Facts: Cal.: 741 | Fat: 64 g | Prot.: 30 g | Net Carbs: 20 g

Ingredients:

- 1 egg
- 1 c. almond flour
- 4 strips bacon—cooked—small bits
- 2 large avocados—lengthwise cuts

For Frying: Olive oil*How to Prepare:*

1. Set the temperature in the fryer to 355°F.
2. Whisk the eggs in one container. Add the flour with the bacon in another.
3. Slice the avocado and dip into the eggs and then the flour mixture.
4. Drizzle oil in the fryer tray and air fry for 10 minutes per side or until they're the way you like them.

Baby Corn

Yields: 4 Servings
Total Time: 18 min.
Nutrition Facts: Cal.: 243 | Fat: 9.6 g | Prot.: 10.3 g | Net Carbs: 8.2 g

Ingredients:

- ½ t. carom seeds
- 1 c. almond flour
- ¼ t. chili powder
- 1 t. garlic powder
- 4 boiled baby ears of corn
- 1 pinch baking soda
- Salt—as desired

How to Prepare:

1. Heat up the Air Fryer (350°F).
2. Whisk the flour, salt, carom seeds, baking soda, garlic powder, and chili powder.
3. Pour a little water to make a batter. Dip the boiled corn in the mixture.
4. Arrange the corn in a foil-lined fryer basket. Cook for 10 minutes.
5. Serve with your favorite entrée and enjoy!

Baked Tomatoes With Feta & Pesto

Yields: 4 Servings
Total Time: 14 min.
Nutrition Facts: Cal.: 246 | Fat: 10.4 g | Prot.: 8.4 g | Net Carbs: 8.6 g

Ingredients for the Pesto:

- 3 tbsp. toasted pine nuts
- 1 clove garlic—toasted
- ½ c. of each:
    - Grated parmesan cheese
- Freshly chopped mix—basil & parsley
- 1 tbsp. olive oil
- 1 pinch of salt

Ingredients for the Feta & Tomatoes:

- 8 oz. feta cheese
- 2 Heirloom tomatoes
- 1 tbsp. olive oil
- A pinch of salt
- ½ c. red onion

How to Prepare:

1. Slice the red onion very thin. Also, cut the cheese and tomatoes into ½-inch slices.
2. Prepare the pesto—omit the salt and oil—using a food processor. Once a thick paste is formed, add the salt, tomatoes, feta, and onion.
3. Program the Air Fryer to 350°F. Place the mixture in the food tray and air fry for 14 minutes.
4. Serve and enjoy with your favorite entrée.

Carrots, Zucchini, & Yellow Squash

Yields: 4 Servings
Total Time: 35 min.
Nutrition Facts: Cal.: 256 | Fat: 9.4 g | Prot.: 7.4 g | Net Carbs: 8.6 g

Ingredients:

- ½ lb. diced carrots
- 6 t. olive oil—divided
- 1 lime—wedges
- 1 lb. of each:
    - Zucchini—¾-inch semi-circles
    - Yellow squash—trimmed
- 1 tbsp. chopped tarragon leaves
- 1 t. sea salt
- ½ t. white pepper

How to Prepare:

1. Program the Air Fryer to 400°F.
2. Trim the stem and roots from the squash and zucchini.
3. Place the carrots in a bowl with 2 teaspoons of oil. Toss and add the carrots to the fryer basket. Prepare for 5 minutes.
4. Place the squash and zucchini in the bowl with the rest of the oil, salt, and pepper.
5. When the carrots are done, fold in the mixture (Step 3). Cook for 30 minutes.
6. Stir occasionally and garnish with the tarragon and lime wedges.

Cheesy Asparagus

Yields: 4 Servings
Total Time: 20 min.
Nutrition Facts: Cal.: 213 | Fat: 18.3 g | Prot.: 7.9 g | Net Carbs: 6.4 g

Ingredients:

- ¼ c. smoked, shredded gouda cheese
- 2 tbsp. Italian seasoning
- ½ c. parmesan cheese
- ½ t. sea salt
- ¼ t. freshly cracked black pepper
- 1 c. heavy cream
- 1 lb. asparagus

How to Prepare:

1. Heat up the Air Fryer to 400°F.
2. Remove a ¼ inch of the bottom of each asparagus.
3. Whisk the heavy cream, Italian seasoning, and parmesan.
4. Place the asparagus in a shallow dish and cover with the mixture.
5. Arrange in the fryer basket for 6 minutes.
6. Serve with the asparagus a sprinkle of cheese, pepper, and salt.

Chili Cumin Squash

Yields: 4 Servings
Total Time: 20 min.
Nutrition Facts: Cal.: 252 | Fat: 10.3 g | Prot.: 8.7 g | Net Carbs: 7.6 g

Ingredients:

- 1 med. butternut squash
- 2/3 c. Greek yogurt
- 1 coriander bunch
- ¼ c. pine nuts
- 2 t. cumin seeds
- 1 pinch chili flakes
- To Taste: Black pepper and salt
- 1 tbsp. olive oil

How to Prepare:

1. Warm up the Air Fryer to 380°F.
2. Cube the squash and combine with the oil and spices in a baking pan.
3. Add them to the fryer for 20 minutes.
4. Toast the pine nuts and enjoy along with the yogurt and a sprinkle of coriander to top it off.

Crispy Black-Eyed Peas

Yields: 6 Servings
Total Time: 15 min.
Nutrition Facts: Cal.: 262 | Fat: 9.4 g | Prot.: 9.2 g | Net Carbs: 8.6 g

Ingredients:

- 1 can (15 oz.) black-eyed peas
- ¼ t. salt
- 1/8 t. of each:
    - Chipotle chili powder
    - Black pepper
- ½ t. chili powder

How to Prepare:

1. Use cold tap water to rinse the beans. Set to the side for now.
2. Preheat the Air Fryer to 360°F.
3. Whisk the spices and add the peas. Stir well.
4. Place in the fryer basket and cook for 10 minutes.
5. Serve with your favorite dinner meal.

Crispy & Spicy Cauliflower

Yields: 4 Servings
Total Time: 20 min.
Nutrition Facts: Cal.: 146 | Fat: 11.8 g | Prot.: 2.7 g | Net Carbs: 9.3 g

Ingredients:

- 4 c. cauliflower florets
- ¼ c. of each:
    - Hot sauce
    - Melted butter
- 1 c. breadcrumbs
1. *How to Prepare:* Warm up the fryer to 350°F.
2. Whisk the hot sauce and melted butter in a mixing bowl.
3. Add the florets in the mixture and toss.
4. Coat the florets with the breadcrumbs and place in the air fryer basket.
5. Air fry for 15 minutes, shaking several times.
6. Enjoy with a favorite dip or sauce but count the extra fat and carbs.

Curried Cauliflower Florets

Yields: 4 Servings
Total Time: 10 min.
Nutrition Facts: Cal.: 275 | Fat: 11.3 g | Prot.: 9.5 g | Net Carbs: 8.6 g

Ingredients:

- 1 c. boiling water
- ¼ c. of each:
    - Golden raisins/Sultanas
    - Pine nuts
- ½ c. olive oil
- ¼ t. salt
- 1 tbsp. curry powder
- 1 head cauliflower—in small florets

How to Prepare:

1. Add the raisins to the cup of boiling water to plump.
2. Set the Air Fryer temperature at 350°F.
3. Toast the nuts in the fryer with the oil for about a minute.
4. Toss the florets with the curry powder and salt in a bowl. Add to the Air Fryer.
5. Cook for 10 minutes. Drain and toss all of the fixings well before serving.

Daikon Fries

Yields: 2 Servings
Total Time: 15 min.
Nutrition Facts: Cal.: 243 | Fat: 27 g | Prot.: 7.3 g | Net Carbs: 1.8 g

Ingredients:

- 1 daikon
- Salt and pepper to taste
- ¼ c. melted coconut oil

How to Prepare:

1. Peel and slice the daikon into fries.
2. Warm the Air Fryer to 450°F.
3. Combine the fixings and toss in the fries to cover.
4. Arrange in the fryer basket and cook for 15 minutes. Shake about ½ way through the cycle. Serve while hot.

Easy Tofu

Yields: 4 Servings
Total Time: 40 min.
Nutrition Facts: Cal.: 89.5 | Fat: 5.6 g | Prot.: 7 g | Net Carbs: 4 g

Ingredients:

- 2 tbsp. sesame oil
- 1 tbsp. cornstarch
- 1 block tofu—1-inch cubes
- 1 t. rice vinegar
- 2 tbsp. soy sauce—(keto-friendly substitute)

How to Prepare:

1. Warm up the fryer ahead of time to 370°F.
2. Combine the oil, vinegar, tofu, and soy sauce substitute of your choice. Toss well and set aside.
3. Toss the cornstarch in a dish and cover the tofu.
4. Place in the fryer basket for 20 minutes. Be sure to shake a couple of times during the cycle.

Grilled Cheesy Corn

Yields: 2 Servings
Total Time: 20 min.
Nutrition Facts: Cal.: 150 | Fat: 10 g | Prot.: 7 g | Net Carbs: 7 g

Ingredients:

- 1 t. olive oil
- 2 t. paprika
- 2 corn-on-the-cobs—whole
- ½ c. grated feta cheese

How to Prepare:

1. Remove the husks and silks. Generously, grease the corn with the oil and give it a sprinkle of the paprika.
2. Warm up the Air Fryer at 392°F.
3. Grill for 15 minutes and place on a serving dish with the cheese as a topping.

Lemony Green Beans

Yields: 4 Servings
Total Time: 16 min.
Nutrition Facts: Cal.: 263 | Fat: 9.2 g | Prot.: 8.7 g | Net Carbs: 8.6 g

Ingredients:

- 1 lemon
- 1 lb. green beans
- ¼ t. extra-virgin olive oil
- Black pepper to your liking
- Sea salt to taste

How to Prepare:

1. Warm up the Air Fryer (400°F).
2. Pour the beans into the fryer basket and give them a squeeze of the lemon.
3. Salt and pepper the beans and cover with oil. Toss well and prepare for 12 minutes. Serve and enjoy immediately.

Onion Rings

Yields: 2 Servings
Total Time: 22 min.
Nutrition Facts: Cal.:364 | Fat: 29.8 g | Prot.: 9.4 g | Net Carbs: 18.7 g

Ingredients:

- 2 tbsp. of each:
    - Coconut flour
    - Grated parmesan cheese
- 1 egg—beaten
- 1 large onion—in ringlets
- Pinch of garlic powder
- Pepper and salt—to taste
- ¼ c. olive oil

How to Prepare:

1. Whisk the flour and spices well and add the grated cheese.
2. Warm up the Air Fryer to 400°F.
3. Whisk the eggs in another dish and add the onion rings. Soak for a minute or so and dip into the flour mixture (Step 1).
4. Prepare in the Air Fryer basket until golden or for 6 minutes on each side.
5. Serve with your favorite entrée or as a quick snack.

Roasted Cauliflower With Raisins & Nuts

Yields: 4 Servings
Total Time: 25 min.
Nutrition Facts: Cal.: 264 | Fat: 26 g | Prot.: 2 g | Net Carbs: 8 g

Ingredients:

- 3½ fl. oz. Olive oil (100 ml—1/3 c. + 2 tbsp.)
- 1 small head of cauliflower—florets
- 2 tbsp. of each:
    - Toasted pine nuts
    - Raisins
- ½ t. salt
- 1 t. curry powder

How to Prepare:

1. Soak the raisins in boiling water and drain. Combine all of the fixings in a bowl, mixing well.
2. Warm up the fryer to 320°F (2 minutes).
3. Combine the fixings in a bowl and add to the basket.
4. Air fry for 15 minutes and enjoy.

Tawa Vegetables

Yields: 4 Servings
Total Time: 35 min.
Nutrition Facts: Cal.: 264 | Fat: 11.3 g | Prot.: 8.7 g | Net Carbs: 10.4 g

Ingredients:

- ¼ c. of each:
    - Potato
    - Okra
    - Taro root
    - Eggplant
- 2 t. garam masala
- 1 t. of each:
    - Red chili powder
    - Amchur powder
- Salt to taste
- For Brushing: Olive oil

How to Prepare:

1. Warm up the Air Fryer to 390°F.
2. Cut the taro root and potatoes into fries and soak in salted water for 10 minutes.
3. Slice the eggplant and okra into four segments.
4. Rinse the potatoes and taro root and pat dry. Combine with the spices, okra, and eggplant.
5. Brush the pan with the oil and cook for 10 minutes. Lower the heat setting to 355°F and cook for 15 more minutes.
6. Enjoy the veggies any way you choose.

Zucchini Fries

Yields: 2 Servings
Total Time: 22 min.
Nutrition Facts: Cal.: 91 | Fat: 5.7 g | Prot.: 5.7 g | Net Carbs: 4.1 g

Ingredients:

- 1 large zucchini
- 2 eggs
- ½ c. flour
- Olive oil
- Salt and pepper to taste
- Cooking spray

How to Prepare:

1. Warm up the Air Fryer (400°F.)
2. Slice the zucchini into fry sticks and shake with the pepper and salt.
3. Coat the fries with the flour and then the egg (beaten in a bowl).

4. Lightly spray the fries with the cooking oil spray and place in the basket.
5. Air fry for 6 minutes per side. Serve with your favorite entrée or as a snack.

Chapter 9: Appetizers

Bacon-Wrapped Chicken

Yields: 3 Servings
Total Time: 13 min.
Nutrition Facts: Cal.: 364 | Fat: 26 g | Prot.: 30.5 g | Net Carbs: 0.6 g

Ingredients:

- 1 breast of chicken
- 6 strips unsmoked bacon
- 1 tbsp. soft garlic cheese

How to Prepare:

1. Slice the chicken into six pieces.
2. Spread the garlic cheese over each bacon strip. Add a piece of chicken to each one. Roll and secure with a toothpick.
3. Prepare the Air Fryer for a couple of minutes. Add the wraps and cook for 15 minutes.

Bacon-Wrapped Prawns

Yields: 4 Servings
Total Time: 30 min.
Nutrition Facts: Cal.: 748 | Fat: 49 g | Prot.: 67 g | Net Carbs: 3 g

Ingredients:

- 1 lb. of each:
    - Bacon slices
    - Peeled prawns

How to Prepare:

1. Warm up the Air Fryer to 390°F.
2. Wrap a bacon slice around each prawn and add to the fryer basket

Prepare for 5 minutes and enjoy.

Charred Shishito Peppers

Yields: 4 Servings
Total Time: 5 min.
Nutrition Facts: Cal.: 243 | Fat: 8.4 g | Prot.: 6.2 g | Net Carbs: 6.3 g

Ingredients:

- 1 t. olive oil
- 1 juiced lemon
- 20 Shishito peppers
- Sea salt to taste

How to Prepare:

1. Warm up the fryer to 390°F.
2. Toss the peppers with the oil and salt. Add them to the basket and cook for 5 minutes.
3. Place on a platter with a squeeze of lemon. Serve and enjoy.

Cheese Balls

Yields: 5 Servings
Total Time: 18 min.
Nutrition Facts: Cal.: 166 | Fat: 12.8 g | Prot.: 9.5 g | Net Carbs: 2.8 g

Ingredients:

- 1 egg
- 8 oz. pkg. mozzarella balls
- ½ c. of each:
    - Coconut flakes
    - Almond flour
- To Taste:
    - Thyme
    - Pepper
    - Paprika

How to Prepare:

1. Program the Air Fryer to 400°F.
2. Whisk the egg in one bowl and combine the spices with flour in a separate bowl.
3. Sprinkle the balls with the coconut flakes and the flour.
4. Freeze the cheese balls for 5 minutes. Add to the fryer for 3 minutes and enjoy!

Herbal Chicken Wings

Yields: 6 Servings
Total Time: 40 min.
Nutrition Facts: Cal.: 673 | Fat: 29 g | Prot.: 88 g | Net Carbs: 9 g

Ingredients:

- 4 lb. chicken wings
- 1 t. chopped thyme
- 6 minced cloves of garlic
- 1 habanero—chopped
- 1 fresh lime—juiced
- ½ tbsp. minced ginger
- 1/3 cup + 2 tbsp. /3. fl. oz. /100 ml vinegar
- 1 tbsp. of each:
    - Brown sugar
    - Olive oil
- 2 tbsp. soy sauce—keto-friendly substitute—your choice
- ¼ t. cinnamon
- ½ t. of each:
    - White pepper
    - Salt

How to Prepare:

1. Program the Air Fryer to 390°F.
2. Combine all of the fixings in a bowl with a lid. Marinate for 2 hours.
3. At that point, transfer the wings to the fryer basket (15 minutes).

Hot Chicken Wings

Yields: 4 Servings
Total Time: 2 hr. 25 min.
Nutrition Facts: Cal.: 587 | Fat: 34.2 g | Prot.: 65.9 g | Net Carbs: 0.5 g

Ingredients:

- 2 lb. chicken wings
- 3 tbsp. melted butter
- ¼ c. hot sauce

Salt*Ingredients for the Finishing Sauce*:

- 4 tbsp. hot sauce

3 tbsp. melted butter*How to Prepare:*

1. In a large mixing container, combine the hot sauce, melted butter, wings, and salt. Coat them well and let the marinate

rest in the fridge for 2 hours.
2. Set the oven temperature to 400°F.
3. Arrange the wings in the fryer basket and fry for 12 minutes.
4. Combine the melted butter and hot sauce.
5. Transfer the wings from the basket and add to the hot sauce. Toss well.
6. Serve and enjoy piping hot!

Onion & Cheese Nuggets

Yields: 4 Servings
Total Time: 1 hr. 17 min.
Nutrition Facts: Cal.: 227 | Fat: 17.3 g | Prot.: 14.2 g | Net Carbs: 4.5 g

Ingredients:

- 1 egg
- 7 oz. grated Edam cheese
- 2 diced spring onions
- Salt and pepper—as desired
- 1 tbsp. of each:
    - Dried thyme
    - Coconut oil

How to Prepare:

1. Program the frying unit to 350°F.
2. Combine all of the fixings (omit the cheese).
3. Make 8 balls out of the mixture and stuff the cheese in the center. Place in the fridge for 1 hour.
4. Whisk the egg and use a pastry brush to coat the nuggets.
5. Place in the Air Fryer for 12 minutes.
6. Enjoy anytime.

Semolina Veggie Cutlets

Yields: 2 Servings
Total Time: 23 min.
Nutrition Facts: Cal.: 252 | Fat: 11.2 g | Prot.: 7.3 g | Net Carbs: 10.3 g

Ingredients:

- Olive oil—for frying
- 1 c. semolina
- To Taste: Salt & Pepper
- 1 ½ c. veggies—for example, peas, green beans, carrots, cauliflower, etc.
- 5 c. milk

How to Prepare:

1. Warm and stir the milk in a saucepan (medium heat). When hot, add the veggies and cook for about 3 minutes. Flavor with the pepper and salt.
2. Add the semolina and cook for another 10 minutes
3. Prepare a baking sheet with a piece of parchment paper. Spread the mixture over the pan to chill in the refrigerator (4 hours).
4. Preheat the Air Fryer to 350°F.
5. Remove the mixture from the fridge and slice into cutlets. Brush with the oil and bake for 10 minutes.
6. Serve with some hot sauce.

Spring Rolls

Yields: 20 Servings
Total Time: 14 min.
Nutrition Facts: Cal.: 267 | Fat: 11.2 g | Prot.: 16.3 g | Net Carbs: 11.2 g

Ingredients:

- 1/3 c. noodles
- 2 tbsp. hot water
- 1 c. of each:
    - Ground Beef
    - Mixed vegetables
- 1 pkg. spring rolls
- 3 minced garlic cloves
- 1 small diced onion
- To Taste: Liquid aminos—soy sauce substitute
- Also Needed: 1 skillet
- Olive oil for brushing

How to Prepare:

1. Add the noodles to hot water to soften. Drain and slice into short segments.
2. Preheat the Air Fryer to 350°F.
3. Warm the skillet (medium heat) and add the oil with the ground beef, garlic, onion, and mixed veggies. If you have a keto-friendly soy sauce (liquid aminos), add that and sauté for 3 minutes or until lightly browned.
4. Place on the countertop and add the prepared noodles. Stir and set to the side for now.
5. Starting diagonally, add the stuffing to the egg roll. Fold the sheet starting at the top and then the sides and brush the final side with the water before rolling the wrap closed.
6. Brush the rolls with oil and arrange in the fryer. Cook for 8 minutes and serve.

Sweet & Sour Chicken Skewers

Yields: 4 Servings
Total Time: 30 min.
Nutrition Facts: Cal.: 268 | Fat: 11 g | Prot.: 33 g | Net Carbs: 5 g

Ingredients:

- 1 lb. chicken tenders
- 4 minced garlic cloves
- 1 tbsp. sesame oil
- ½ t. minced ginger
- ¼ t. pepper
- 3½ fl. oz. or 1/3 cup + 2 tbsp.

How to Prepare:

1. Heat up the Air Fryer to 390°F.
2. Combine all of the fixings in a mixing container.
3. Skewer the chicken and add them to the marinade for 2 hours.
4. At that time, air fry for 18 minutes. Serve when crispy and hot.

Zucchini Roll-Ups

Yields: 2 Servings
Total Time: 10 min.
Nutrition Facts: Cal.: 243 | Fat: 8.7 g | Prot.: 6.5 g | Net Carbs: 6.4 g

Ingredients:

- 1 c. goat cheese
- 3 zucchinis
- Sea salt to taste
- ¼ t. black pepper

1 tbsp. olive oil*How to Prepare:*

1. Program the Air Fryer to 390°F.
2. Slice the zucchini thin—lengthwise. Brush each strip with the oil.
3. Mix the cheese with the salt and pepper. Scoop onto the zucchini strips, roll, and fasten with a toothpick.
4. Arrange in the fryer and prepare for 5 minutes. Yummy!

Snacks

Coconut Chips

Yields: 2 Servings
Total Time: 5 min.
Nutrition Facts: Cal.: 261 | Fat: 9.2 g | Prot.: 6.2 g | Net Carbs: 7.3 g

Ingredients:

- 2 c. shredded coconut—large pieces
- 1 tbsp. chili powder
- 1/3 t. liquid stevia

How to Prepare:

1. Warm up the Air Fryer to 390°F.
2. Combine all of the fixings and add to the fryer.
3. Set the timer for 5 minutes and enjoy!

Crispy Kale Chips

Yields: 2 Servings
Total Time: 10 min.
Nutrition Facts: Cal.: 86 | Fat: 7 g | Prot.: 1.7 g | Net Carbs: 5 g

Ingredients:

- 1 head cabbage
- 1 tbsp. olive oil
- 1 t. soy sauce—*Note:* keto approved/tamari/another substitute

How to Prepare:

1. Rinse the kale, dry, and add to a mixing bowl with the rest of the fixings.
2. Set the fryer at 200°F and add the kale. Toss ½ way through the cycle.
3. Serve anytime.

Onion Pakora

Yields: 6 Servings
Total Time: 6 min.
Nutrition Facts: Cal.: 253 | Fat: 12.2 g | Prot.: 7.6 g | Net Carbs: 11.4 g

Ingredients:

- ¼ c. rice flour
- 1 c. graham flour
- 2 t. olive oil
- Salt to taste
- ¼ t. of each:
    - Carom
    - Turmeric powder
- 1 tbsp. freshly chopped coriander
- 2 green chili peppers—finely diced
- 2 t. olive oil
- 1/8 t. chili powder

How to Prepare:

1. Warm up the Air Fryer to 350°F.
2. Combine the rice and graham flour and mix with the oil. Add small amounts of water to make a doughy consistency.
3. Blend in the onions, peppers, carom, coriander, turmeric, and chili powder.
4. Roll the mixture into small balls and arrange in the fryer. Cook for 8 minutes and enjoy with some hot sauce or other spices you may like.

Pineapple Sticks With Yogurt Dip

Yields: 2 Servings
Total Time: 10 min.
Nutrition Facts: Cal.: 246 | Fat: 8.4 g | Prot.: 6.3 g | Net Carbs: 7.2 g

Ingredients:

- ½ of a pineapple
- ¼ c. dried coconut

Ingredients for the Dip:

- 1 c. vanilla yogurt
- 1 fresh mint sprig

How to Prepare:

1. Warm up the fryer to 390°F.
2. Slice the pineapple into sticks and dip in the coconut.
3. Place in the Air Fryer basket for 10 minutes.
4. Prepare the dip and dice the mint leaves. Combine and serve with the tasty dip anytime.

Roasted Cashews

Yields: 5 Servings
Total Time: 15 min.
Nutrition Facts: Cal.: 272 | Fat: 22 g | Prot.: 7 g | Net Carbs: 14 g

Ingredients:

- 1 2/3 c. cashews
- 1 t. of each:
    - Olive oil
    - Coriander powder
    - Red chili powder
- ½ t. of each:
    - Black pepper
    - Salt

How to Prepare:

1. Preheat the Air Fryer at 248°F.
2. Combine all of the components in a mixing container.
3. Toss well and add to the fryer basket. Air fry until lightly browned (10 minutes).

Spiced Nuts

Yields: 3 Cups
Total Time: 15 min.
Nutrition Facts: Cal.: 4688 | Fat: 424 g | Prot.: 88 g | Net Carbs: 153 g

Ingredients:

- 1 beaten egg white
- ¼ t. ground cloves
- ½ t. ground cinnamon
- Pinch of cayenne pepper
- Salt to your liking
- 1 c. of each:
    - Pecan halves
    - Cashews
    - Almonds

How to Prepare:

1. Mix the spices with the egg white.
2. Warm up the fryer to 300°F.
3. Toss the nuts into the mixture and shake.
4. Prepare in the Air Fryer for 25 minutes, stirring several times.
5. Enjoy every morsel!

Sweet Potato Chips

Yields: 2 Servings
Total Time: 15 min.
Nutrition Facts: Cal.: 253 | Fat: 11.2 g | Prot.: 6.5 g | Net Carbs: 8.4 g

Ingredients:

- 2 large sweet potatoes
- Salt to taste
- 2 tbsp. olive oil
- Also Needed: 1 mandoline slicer

How to Prepare:

1. Warm up the Air Fryer (350°F).
2. Slice the potatoes with the mandoline and add to a large bowl. Add the oil and stir to coat.

Place in the fryer for about 15 minutes or until crispy the way you like them.

Chapter 10: Lunch Recipes

These are just a few of the tasty lunchtime recipes you can enjoy while staying on your ketogenic diet.

Avocado & Turkey Burrito

Yields: 2 Servings
Total Time: 15 min.
Nutrition Facts: Cal.: 289 | Fat: 11.2 g | Prot.: 12.3 g | Net Carbs: 9.7 g

Ingredients:

- 4 eggs
- Pepper & Salt—to taste
- 4 tbsp. salsa
- 8 slices cooked turkey breast
- ½ c. sliced avocado
- ¼ c. mozzarella cheese—grated
- ½ sliced red bell pepper
- 2 tortillas

How to Prepare:

1. Whisk the eggs with the pepper and salt. Spray the Air Fryer tray with some nonstick cooking oil. Add the eggs.
2. Prepare at 390°F for 5 minutes. Scrape the bowl and add the eggs to the tortillas.
3. Layer the turkey, avocado, peppers, cheese, and salsa. Roll it up slowly.
4. Spray the fryer and arrange the burritos in the basket. Prepare for 5 minutes.
5. Serve warm and enjoy when you're in a hurry.

Beef & Potato

Yields: 4 Servings
Total Time: 25 min.
Nutrition Facts: Cal.: 296 | Fat: 12.2 g | Prot.: 16.3 g | Net Carbs: 11.8 g

Ingredients:

- 1 lb. ground beef
- 3 c. mashed potatoes
- 2 eggs
- 2 tbsp. garlic powder
- 1 c. sour cream
- To Taste: Freshly cracked black pepper
- Pinch of salt

How to Prepare:

1. Preheat the Air Fryer to 390°F.
2. Combine all of the fixings in a mixing bowl and place in a heat-safe dish.
3. Place in the fryer for 2 minutes.
4. Enjoy when you want a bit more than a sandwich for lunch.

Beef Roll-Ups

Yields: 4 Servings
Total Time: 20 min.
Nutrition Facts: Cal.: 282 | Fat: 12.3 g | Prot.: 16.3 g | Net Carbs: 9.8 g

Ingredients:

- 3 tbsp. pesto
- 2 lb. beef flank steak
- ¾ c. fresh baby spinach
- 3 oz. roasted red bell peppers
- 6 slices provolone cheese
- To Taste: Sea salt and Pepper

How to Prepare:

1. Warm the Air Fryer to 400°F.
2. Slice the steak open (not all the way through). Spread the pesto over the meat.
3. Layer the peppers, cheese, and spinach about ¾ of the way into the meat.
4. Roll it up with toothpicks. Give it a sprinkle of the pepper and salt.
5. Air fry for 14 minutes—rotating halfway through the cycle.
6. When the timer buzzes, let the meat rest for about 10 minutes.
7. Slice and serve.

Beef Stew

Yields: 6 Servings
Total Time: 38 min.
Nutrition Facts: Cal.: 144 | Fat: 5.8 g | Prot.: 15.7 g | Net Carbs: 5.1 g

Ingredients:

- 2 t. butter
- 10 oz. beef short ribs
- ½ t. chili flakes
- ¼ t. salt
- 1 t. turmeric
- 1 c. chicken stock
- ½ onion
- 1 green pepper
- 4 oz. of each:
    - Kale
    - Green peas

How to Prepare:

1. Program the Air Fryer to 360°F.
2. Add the butter to melt in the fryer basket and place the ribs.
3. Sprinkle with the chili flakes, salt, and turmeric. Cook for 15 minutes.
4. Remove the seeds and chop the green pepper and kale. Dice the onion.
5. When the timer buzzes, pour in the stock along with the peppers and onions. Sprinkle with the peas and add the peeled garlic clove.
6. Stir well and add the chopped kale. Cook for 8 more minutes.
7. Let the stew steep for a short while to blend all the delicious flavors.
8. Serve and relax.

Beef & Bacon Taco Rolls

Yields: 2 Servings
Total Time: 25 min.
Nutrition Facts: Cal.: 286 | Fat: 12.5 g | Prot.: 16.6 g | Net Carbs: 10.2 g

Ingredients:

- 2 c. ground beef
- To Taste—with the beef taco spices:
    - Garlic powder
    - Chili powder
    - Black pepper
- ½ c. bacon bits
- 1 c. of each:
    - Tomato salsa
    - Shredded Monterey Jack Cheese
- 4 turmeric coconut wraps/your choice

How to Prepare:

1. Heat the fryer to 390°F.
2. Season the beef with the spices. Add all of the fixings to the wraps.
3. Roll up the wraps and arrange them in the Air Fryer.
4. Air fry for 15 minutes and serve.

Cheeseburger Patties

Yields: 6 Servings
Total Time: 15 min.
Nutrition Facts: Cal.: 253 | Fat: 14 g | Prot.: 29 g | Net Carbs: 0.4 g

Ingredients:

- 1 lb. ground beef
- Salt
- Black pepper
- 6 slices cheddar cheese

How to Prepare:

1. Program the Air Fryer. Combine the fixings and mix well.
2. Shape into six burgers.
3. Air fry for 10 minutes and enjoy!

Chicken Curry

Yields: 4 Servings
Total Time: 25 min.
Nutrition Facts: Cal.: 275 | Fat: 15.7 g | Prot.: 25.6 g | Net Carbs: 5.9 g

Ingredients:

- 1 lb. chicken breast—no skin or bones
- 1 t. olive oil
- 1 onion
- 2 t. minced garlic
- 1 tbsp. of each:
    - Lemongrass
    - Apple cider vinegar
- ½ c. each:
    - Chicken stock
    - Coconut milk
- 2 tbsp. curry paste

How to Prepare:

1. Preheat the fryer to 365°F.
2. Chop the chicken into cubes. Peel and dice the onion and combine in the Air Fryer basket. Cook for 5 minutes.
3. Remove and add the rest of the fixings. Mix well and cook for another 10 minutes.
4. Serve and enjoy for lunch for a quick and healthy meal.

Corn Beef

Yields: 3 Servings
Total Time: 29 min.
Nutrition Facts: Cal.: 310 | Fat: 10.8 g | Prot.: 46.4 g | Net Carbs: 3 g

Ingredients:

- 1 finely sliced onion
- 1 c. water
- 1 lb. minced beef
- 1 t. of each:
    - Black pepper
    - Butter
- ¼ t. cayenne pepper
- ½ t. ground paprika

How to Prepare:

1. Warm the Air Fryer to 400°F.
2. Peel and slice the onion. Pour water into the pizza tray and add the onion. Sprinkle with the spices. Stir and cook for 4 minutes.
3. Remove from the tray and add the minced garlic. Stir and add back to the Air Fryer. Continue cooking for 7 minutes. Carefully, stir in the beef and cook for 8 more minutes.
4. Remove from the fryer and add to the serving plates.

Grilled Cheese

Yields: 2 Servings
Total Time: 15 min.
Nutrition Facts: Cal.: 608 | Fat: 57 g | Prot.: 14 g | Net Carbs: 9 g

Ingredients:

- ½ c. melted butter
- 4 slices bread
- 1 c. shredded cheddar cheese

How to Prepare:

1. Butter all slices of bread. Assemble each sandwich and arrange in the basket.
2. Set the Air Fryer at 355°F.
3. Prepare for 7 minutes and serve right away.

Herbed Shredded Beef

Yields: 8 Servings
Total Time: 37 min.
Nutrition Facts: Cal.: 265 | Fat: 14 g | Prot.: 32.4 g | Net Carbs: 1.0 g

Ingredients:

- 1 t. of each:
    - Thyme
    - Salt
    - Ground black pepper
    - Mustard
    - Dried dill
- 2 lb. beef steak
- 4 c. chicken stock
- 3 tbsp. butter
- 1 peeled garlic clove
- 1 bay leaf

How to Prepare:

1. Heat the Air Fryer in advance (350°F).
2. Whisk the egg and add the stevia, baking powder, and butter.
3. Reserve 1 teaspoon of the almond flour and add the rest to the mixture. Knead until it's smooth and not sticky.
4. Line the fryer basket with parchment paper and add the prepared crust. Flatten and place the berries on top. Sprinkle with (1 teaspoon) the almond flour.
5. Prepare the pie in the Air Fryer for 20 minutes and remove when it's golden brown.
6. Chill and slice for your awaiting guests. Add a tasty salad and enjoy.

Mozzarella Turkey Rolls

Yields: 4 Servings
Total Time: 15 min.
Nutrition Facts: Cal.: 296 | Fat: 12.4 g | Prot.: 16.2 g | Net Carbs: 10.2 g

Ingredients:

- 1 sliced tomato
- 4 slices turkey breast
- ½ c. freshly chopped basil
- 1 c. sliced mozzarella
- 4 chive shoots—for tying

How to Prepare:

1. Warm up the Air Fryer to 390F.
2. On each slice of turkey, add a slice of cheese, tomato, and basil.
3. Roll up each one and tie them with the chive shoot.
4. Add to the fryer for 10 minutes. Prepare and serve warm.

Pita Bread Pizza

Yields: 1 Serving
Total Time: 8 min.
Nutrition Facts: Cal.: 249 | Fat: 15 g | Prot.: 14 g | Net Carbs: 13 g

Ingredients:

- 1 pita bread
- 1 t. olive oil
- 1 tbsp. pizza sauce—keto-friendly
- ¼ c. shredded mozzarella cheese
- ½ t. minced garlic
- 1 tbsp. sliced onion
- 7 pepperoni slices
- ¼ c. sausage

How to Prepare:

1. Set the Air Fryer to 350°F.
2. Prepare the pita bread with the sauce. Toss on the sausage, onion, and pepperoni.
3. Sprinkle with the cheese and garlic.
4. Drizzle a little of the oil over the pizza and arrange on the trivet in the Air Fryer.
5. Air fry for 6 minutes and serve right out of the cooker.

Roast Beef for Sandwiches

Yields: 6 Servings
Total Time: 1 hr. 5 min.
Nutrition Facts: Cal.: 304 | Fat: 12.8 g | Prot.: 16.8 g | Net Carbs: 11.7 g

Ingredients:

- ½ t. of each:
    - Oregano
    - Garlic powder
- 1 t. dried thyme
- 1 tbsp. olive oil
- 2 lb. round roast

How to Prepare:

1. Heat up the Air Fryer to 330°F.
2. Combine the spices. Brush the oil over the beef and rub in the spice mixture.
3. Add to a baking dish and place in the fryer for 30 minutes. Turn it over and continue cooking for 25 more minutes.
4. Let it rest for a few minutes before slicing.
5. Serve on your choice of keto-friendly bread or eat it as it is.

Salmon Croquettes

Yields: 4 Servings
Total Time: 15 min.
Nutrition Facts: Cal.: 363 | Fat: 27 g | Prot.: 24 g | Net Carbs: 6 g

Ingredients:

- 1 lb. (can) red salmon
- 1 c. breadcrumbs
- 1/3 c. vegetable oil
- ½ bunch chopped parsley
- 2 eggs

How to Prepare:

1. Set the Air Fryer at 392°F.
2. Drain and mash the salmon. Combine with the beaten eggs and parsley.
3. In another dish, mix the oil and breadcrumbs.
4. Make 16 croquettes with the mixture and coat with the breadcrumbs.
5. Arrange in the preheated basket for 7 minutes.
6. Enjoy for lunch or any other time you want something new.

Stuffed Mushrooms

Yields: 3 Servings
Total Time: 15 min.
Nutrition Facts: Cal.: 271 | Fat: 18.3 g | Prot.: 19 g | Net Carbs: 8 g

Ingredients:

- 3 Portobello mushrooms
- 1 t. minced garlic
- 1 med. diced onion
- 3 tbsp. grated mozzarella cheese
- 1 tbsp. olive oil
- 2 slices chopped ham
- 1 diced tomato
- 1 diced green pepper
- ½ t. sea salt
- ¼ t. pepper

How to Prepare:

1. Warm up the Air Fryer to 320°F.
2. Wash, dry, and remove the stems from the mushrooms. Drizzle with oil and set aside for now.
3. Combine the pepper, salt, cheese, tomato, onion, garlic, bell peppers, and ham and stuff them into the mushroom caps.
4. Add the mushrooms to the fryer for 8 minutes.
5. Serve with your favorite entrée.

Chapter 11: Dinner Choices

Enjoy an evening with friends and family with a plate of delicious seafood or other healthy selection from this segment.

Fish & SeafoodCoconut Shrimp

Yields: 3 Servings
Total Time: 20 min.
Nutrition Facts: Cal.: 174 | Fat: 9 g | Prot.: 14 g | Net Carbs: 7 g

Ingredients:

- 12 large shrimp
- 1 c. of each:
    - Gluten-free flour
    - Gluten-free breadcrumbs
    - Egg white
    - Coconut—Unsweetened + Dried
- 1 tbsp. cornstarch

How to Prepare:

1. Program the Air Fryer to 350°F.
2. Preparation Steps: Prepare a shallow platter and combine the breadcrumbs and coconut. In another bowl, mix the cornstarch and flour. Add the egg to a small bowl.
3. Coat the shrimp with the egg white, flour, and lastly, the breadcrumbs.
4. Arrange in the fryer basket for 10 minutes.
5. Serve with your favorite sides or enjoy as a quick snack.

Cod Sticks

Yields: 5 Servings
Total Time: 20 min.
Nutrition Facts: Cal.: 205 | Fat: 5 g | Prot.: 26 g | Net Carbs: 11 g

Ingredients:

- 3 tbsp. milk
- 2 large eggs
- 2 c. breadcrumbs
- ¼ t. salt
- ½ t. black pepper
- 1 c. almond flour
- 1 lb. cod

How to Prepare:

1. Program the Air Fryer to 350°F.
2. Prepare 3 bowls: 1 with the milk and eggs, 1 with the pepper, salt, and breadcrumbs, and another with almond flour.
3. Dip the sticks in the flour, egg mixture, and the breadcrumbs.
4. Place in the basket for 12 minutes shaking halfway through the air frying process.
5. Serve with your favorite sauce (add the carbs).

Creamy Salmon

Yields: 2 Servings
Total Time: 20 min.
Nutrition Facts: Cal.: 426 | Fat: 25 g | Prot.: 41 g | Net Carbs: 13 g

Ingredients:

- Pinch of salt
- ¾ lb. (6 pieces) salmon
- 1 tbsp. of each:
    - Olive oil
    - Chopped dill
- 3 tbsp. sour cream
- 1.76 oz. plain yogurt (50 g)

How to Prepare:

1. Set the temperature on the Air Fryer to 285°F.
2. Shake the salt over the salmon and add them to the fryer basket with the olive oil. Air fry for 10 minutes.
3. Whisk the yogurt, dill, and salt.
4. Serve the salmon with the sauce with your favorite sides.

Fish Nuggets

Yields: 4 Servings
Total Time: 30 min.
Nutrition Facts: Cal.: 334 | Fat: 20 g | Prot.: 25 g | Net Carbs: 10 g

Ingredients:

- 1 lb. cod fillet
- 3 eggs
- 4 tbsp. olive oil
- 1 c. of each:
    - Almond flour
    - Gluten-free breadcrumbs
- 1 t. salt

How to Prepare:

1. Set the temperature of the Air Fryer at 390°F.
2. Cut the cod into nuggets.
3. Prepare three dishes. Beat the eggs in one. Combine the salt, oil, and breadcrumbs in another. The last one will be almond flour.
4. Cover each of the nuggets with the flour, a dip in the eggs, and the breadcrumbs.
5. Arrange the prepared nuggets in the basket and air fry for 20 minutes. Serve.

Grilled Prawns/Shrimp

Yields: 4 Servings
Total Time: 15 min.
Nutrition Facts: Cal.: 137 | Fat: 4 g | Prot.: 20 g | Net Carbs: 3 g

Ingredients:

- 8 medium shrimp/prawns
- 1 tbsp. melted butter
- 1 rosemary sprig
- Pepper & Salt—to your liking
- 3 minced garlic cloves

How to Prepare:

1. Combine all of the components in a mixing bowl. Toss well and arrange in the fryer basket.
2. Air fry the prawns for 7 minutes and serve.

Other Tasty Meals Beef, lamb, and chicken will tempt your taste buds in this segment!

Beef Schnitzel

Yields: 1 Serving
Total Time: 20 min.
Nutrition Facts: Cal.: 469 | Fat: 35 g | Prot.: 29 g | Net Carbs: 12 g

Ingredients:

- 2 tbsp. olive oil
- 1 thin beef schnitzel
- ½ c. gluten-free breadcrumbs
- 1 egg

How to Prepare:

1. Warm up the Air Fryer for a couple of minutes (356°F).
2. Combine the oil and breadcrumbs in a shallow bowl. Whisk the egg in another mixing bowl.
3. Dip the beef into the egg and then the breadcrumbs. Arrange in the preheated basket of the Air Fryer.
4. Fry for 12 minutes and serve.

Lamb Meatballs

Yields: 4 Servings
Total Time: 30 min.
Nutrition Facts: Cal.: 297 | Fat: 13 g | Prot.: 41.3 g | Net Carbs: 0.8 g

Ingredients:

- 1 egg white
- 1 lb. ground lamb
- 4 oz. turkey
- ½ t. salt
- 2 minced garlic cloves
- 2 tbsp. parsley
- 1 tbsp. of each—chopped:
    - Coriander
    - Mint
- 1 tbsp. olive oil

How to Prepare:

1. Heat the Air Fryer to 320°F.
2. Combine all of the fixings in a mixing container. Blend well and shape into small meatballs.
3. Arrange in the Air Fryer and prepare for 15 minutes.
4. When ready, pair it up with your favorite sauce or side dish; just remember to count those carbs.

Steak—Medium-Rare

Yields: 1 Serving
Total Time: 11 min.
Nutrition Facts: Cal.: 445 | Fat: 21 g | Prot.: 59.6 g | Net Carbs: 0.0 g

Ingredients:

- 1 (1 ½-inch) beef steak
- Pepper and salt—to taste
- Olive oil

How to Prepare:

1. Warm up the fryer to 350°F.
2. Oil the steak and season with the pepper and salt.
3. Arrange the prepared beef in the tray and cook for 3 minutes per side.

Whole Chicken: Rotisserie Style

Yields: 4 Servings
Total Time: 1 hr. 5 min.
Nutrition Facts: Cal.: 1306 | Fat: 88 g | Prot.: 121 g | Net Carbs: 0.0 g

Ingredients:

- Olive oil—as needed
- 1 (6-7 lb.) whole chicken
- Seasoned salt
- *Note:* Under 6 lb. for a 3.7-quart Air Fryer

How to Prepare:

1. Clean and dry the chicken and coat with the oil. Season with the salt.
2. Arrange the chicken in the Air Fryer—skin-side down.
3. Cook at 350°F for 30 minutes. Turn it over and continue cooking for another 30 minutes.
4. Serve any way you like it.

Chapter 12: Dessert Temptations

When nothing but something sweet will do, find a tasty treat here!

Blackberry Pie

Yields: 8 Servings
Total Time: 35 min.
Nutrition Facts: Cal.: 60 | Fat: 3.5 g | Prot.: 1.7 g | Net Carbs: 1.6 g

Ingredients:

- 1 large egg
- 2 tbsp. unsalted butter
- 1 tbsp. baking powder
- 1 scoop stevia
- 1 c. almond flour
- ½ c. blackberries
- *Also Needed:* Parchment paper

How to Prepare:

1. Heat up the Air Fryer to 350°F.
2. Whisk the egg and add the butter, stevia, and baking powder.
3. Reserve 1 teaspoon of the flour and add the rest to the mixture. Knead until smooth—not sticky.
4. Cover the fryer basket with the paper and add the dough. Flatten into the shape of a pie crust and add the berries. Sprinkle with the rest of the almond flour on top.
5. Air fry until it's golden (20 minutes) Chill before slicing to serve.

Cheesecake

Yields: 6 Servings
Total Time: 41 min.
Nutrition Facts: Cal.: 307 | Fat: 30.4 g | Prot.: 6.6 g | Net Carbs: 2.6 g

Ingredients:

- ½ c. almonds
- 6 tbsp. soft butter
- 1 tbsp. stevia
- ½ t. vanilla extract
- 1 c. cream cheese
- 2 eggs
- 2 tbsp. swerve
- ¼ t. cinnamon
- 1 t. lemon zest
- *Also Needed:* Parchment paper

How to Prepare:

1. Combine the butter, vanilla, stevia, and sliced almonds.
2. Cover the Air Fryer tray with the paper and add the cheesecake crust (Step 1).
3. Combine the cinnamon, swerve, lemon zest, and cream cheese.
4. Use a hand mixer to prepare the eggs until soft and fluffy. Pour the cream cheese mixture over the almond crust.
5. Set the Air Fryer temperature to 310°F. Cook for 16 minutes. When done, chill for at least 2 hours.
6. Then, slice and enjoy!

Chocolate Chip Cookies

Yields: 5 Servings
Total Time: 30 min.
Nutrition Facts: Cal.: 157 | Fat: 15.2 g | Prot.: 3 g | Net Carbs: 3.2 g

Ingredients:

- 1 egg
- 2 tbsp. dark chocolate chips
- 3 tbsp. of each:
    - Unsalted butter
    - Crushed macadamia nuts
- 1 c. almond flour
- ½ t. vanilla extract
- 1 t. stevia
- ¼ t. of each:
    - Baking powder
    - Salt

How to Prepare:

1. Whisk the eggs and blend in the butter and flour.
2. Mix in the rest of the fixings and knead the dough.
3. Make 5 balls for the cookie dough.
4. Program the Air Fryer to 360°F for a minute or so to warm up.
5. Arrange the cookies in the fryer and flatten (just a little) and cook for 15 minutes.
6. Cool slightly and enjoy. There is nothing like a piping hot cookie right out of the cooker!

Green Avocado Pudding

Yields: 3 Servings
Total Time: 13 min.
Nutrition Facts: Cal.: 199 | Fat: 19.3 g | Prot.: 2.2 g | Net Carbs: 2.6 g

Ingredients:

- 1 pitted avocado
- 5 tbsp. almond milk
- 3 t. stevia
- ¼ t of each:
    - Vanilla extract
    - Salt
- 1 tbsp. cocoa powder

How to Prepare:

1. Warm up the Air Fryer for a couple of minutes at 360°F.
2. Peel and mash the avocado and combine with the milk, salt, vanilla extract, and stevia. Stir in the cocoa powder.
3. Prepare in the Air Fryer for 3 minutes.
4. Chill well and serve.

Sweet Bacon Cookies

Yields: 6 Servings
Total Time: 17 min.
Nutrition Facts: Cal.: 109 | Fat: 8.8g | Prot.: 5.2 g | Net Carbs: 3 g

Ingredients:

- 5 tbsp. keto-friendly peanut butter
- 4 slices cooked, chopped bacon
- 3 tbsp. swerve
- ¼ t. of each:
    - Ground ginger
    - Baking soda
- ½ t. vanilla extract

How to Prepare:

1. Warm up the Air Fryer to 350°F.
2. Combine all of the fixings—bacon last—in a large mixing bowl.
3. Once it is consistent, make it into a log. Break it apart into six segments. Roll the balls and gently flatten.
4. Arrange the cookies in the fryer basket and prepare for 7 minutes.

Chill when done and enjoy.

Conclusion

Thanks again for having the patience to enjoy your copy of the *Keto Diet Air Fryer Cookbook: Fried Food is No Longer a Problem! Little Oil, you Lose Weight and a Lot of Health!* You will discover all of the reasons you will enjoy these delicious recipes once you know how convenient and energy efficient meal planning is when you own an Air Fryer. The ability to grill, bake, and fry make the Air Fryer a "must have" for any kitchen.

There's no recommendation for the amount of oil you need to add (unless shown in the recipes given). It will depend greatly on the types of food and your taste. You may cook many items without oil. You now see how easy it can be to measure out the ingredients and follow the step-by-step information provided for each of the tasty recipes that will keep you in the state of ketosis. All you need to do is gather a shopping list of what you need to become ketogenic and head to the superstore for supplies.The meal combinations are flexible, and you will soon discover what you have been missing out of life with so much less time consumed in food prep. You know this is a great addition to your cookbook resources. It will surely be frequently used as you plan your weekly meal plans.If you have a dog, prepare a batch of these:

Air-Fried Puppy Poppers

Yields: 50 Treats
Total Time: 12-15 min.*Ingredients:*1 c. peanut butter
½ c. unsweetened applesauce
1 t. baking powder
2 c. oats
1 c. flour

How to Prepare:

1. Mix the peanut butter and applesauce in a bowl until creamy.
2. Toss in the oats, baking powder, and flour. When smooth, roll out the dough. Shape into teaspoon-sized balls.
3. Prepare the air fryer to reach 350°F.
4. Coat the bottom/bucket of the fryer basket with a little oil.
5. Arrange 8-12 of the balls in the basket and cook for 8 minutes. Turn halfway through. Continue with the process with the batter until all are done. Cool completely before storing.
6. The poppers will stay fresh for up to two weeks.

Enjoy!

Made in the USA
Middletown, DE
24 October 2018